The
Kissinger Study
of
Southern Africa

National Security
Study Memorandum 39

(SECRET)

The Kissinger Study
of
Southern Africa

National Security Study Memorandum 39

(SECRET)

Edited and Introduced by
MOHAMED A. EL-KHAWAS AND BARRY COHEN

Preface by Edgar Lockwood

LAWRENCE HILL & COMPANY
Westport, Connecticut

Library of Congress Cataloging in Publication Data

The Kissinger Study of Southern Africa

    Includes bibliographical references.
    1. United States — Foreign relations — Africa, Southern.
    2. Africa, Southern — Foreign relations — United States.

JX1428.A37K57   327.73'068   76-18043
ISBN 0-88208-071-7
ISBN 0-88208-072-5 pbk.

Preface copyright © 1976 by Edgar Lockwood
Part I copyright © 1976 by Mohamed A. El-Khawas and Barry Cohen

Library of Congress Catalog Card Number: LC: 76-18043
ISBN: 0-88208-071-7 (cloth edition)
ISBN: 0-88208-072-5 (paperback edition)

First Edition, September, 1976

1 2 3 4 5 6 7 8 9 10

Lawrence Hill & Company, Publishers, Inc.
Manufactured in the United States of America

DESIGNED BY RAY FREIMAN

PUBLISHER'S NOTE

This book contains the complete unabridged text of the study prepared by the United States National Security Council Interdepartmental Group for Africa in response to National Security Study Memorandum 39.

In connection with the publication of this document, the following exchange of letters between the publisher and the State Department took place:

LAWRENCE HILL&CO.
Publishers, inc.   24 BURR FARMS ROAD / WESTPORT, CONNECTICUT 06880 / (203) 226-9392

September 18, 1975

Dr. Henry A. Kissinger
Department of State
Washington, DC 20520

Dear Dr. Kissinger:

Can you or one of your deputies inform me as to
whether or not National Security Study Memorandum
39 on Southern Africa is still classified as
secret? My firm is considering the publication
of a book which would reprint the Memorandum in
full along with an analysis of it by an African
scholar.

Since Memorandum 39 has recently been published
in a book in England and is available in the US,
I assume that it is no longer restricted--but I
would like assurance from your office before de-
ciding how to proceed.

In connection with the book I am contemplating,
it would also be helpful to receive any more
recent analyses of the situation in Africa prepared
by the National Security Council, the State Department or the CIA since Memorandum 39 reflects the
situation in Africa before the Portuguese colonies
achieved their freedom.

I look forward with interest to receiving your
reply.

Sincerely,

Lawrence Hill

Lawrence Hill

LH:spr

November 4, 1975

Dear Mr. Hill:

I have been asked to respond to your letter of September 18, 1975 regarding the classification of National Security Study Memorandum No. 39. After a review in response to requests under the Freedom of Information Act, it has been determined that this document remains classified and thus is unavailable for publication.

With regard to your request for recent analyses of the situation in Africa, such documents as are available to the public may be procured from the Department of State's Office of Public Affairs. If you wish to write that office, the address is:

> Ms. Susan M. Haufe
> Public Inquiries Division (PA/MS/PI)
> Room 5821 - New State Building
> Department of State
> Washington, D.C. 20520.

Sincerely,

Jeanne W. Davis
Staff Secretary

Mr. Lawrence Hill
Lawrence Hill & Co.
24 Burr Farms Rd.
Westport, Connecticut 06880

Table of Contents

Preface

The end of white rule in southern Africa draws closer day by day. The collapse of the Portuguese colonial regime, brought about by the guerilla liberation armies, has shortened the time frame within which we look at the future. We are bound to feel now that the schedule will be written in years, not in decades as one might once have felt. The domino theory, while it has no validity as a forecast of white collapse, still has some use as a projection of a series of linked victories. First the crisis will come in Zimbabwe (Rhodesia), and white rule by a 5-percent minority will be ended; next it will be the turn of Namibians to liberate themselves; at length, by processes that can be intuitively felt but not known, South Africa itself, the heart of apartheid's monster, will fall.

For the United States government, what was once a matter of leisurely planning and haphazard rationalization of contradictory interests and political postures becomes a question of moment and urgency, full of allegedly global consequence. Secretary Kissinger's intervention in Angola makes it plain that, for him, the forces of communism, which had been defeated in the Congo in the sixties, are winning new and dangerous influence in central and southern Africa, not only destabilizing the region but also threatening a momentous shift in the world balance of power. Why this sequential conclusion should necessarily follow is a matter of puzzlement as well as almost daily comment. For this reason, if for no other, it is urgent that all Americans interested in these issues read this timely book. In it we have the original text, unexpurgated and unabridged, of a secret study memorandum prepared at Dr. Kissinger's direction in 1969 in order to furnish the National Security Council with options for United States policy toward southern Africa.

But isn't this by now outdated, and in any case, isn't it just a study paper? Was policy actually changed as a result of this study?

Of course, the memorandum is dated. It was written before the Portuguese coup, before the defeat of the United States in Vietnam, before the Watergate scandals, before the Arabs imposed a new price for energy on the West, before the deterioration of capitalist economies because of inflation, scarcities of mineral supplies and energy, loss of productivity, etc., – and before the Angolan war. The facts of the memorandum can be brought up to date, as Mohamed El-Khawas and Barry Cohen have done in their important and useful introduction. With this accomplished, it will be seen that the "tangible interests" which formed the foundation of US policy under any of the five options elaborated in the memorandum are much greater in the mid-seventies than they were in 1969.

By the end of 1974, US direct investment in South Africa had risen to 40 percent of all US investment in Africa from a level of 25.8 percent in 1968. At the same time, trade had doubled without diminishing the two-to-one favorable balance. Arguing from the results and the foreseeable trend, we can see that Option 2 has in fact amounted to an encouragement of US investment and trade in South Africa.

State Department spokesmen tried to play down the importance of NSSM 39 when it was first revealed in detail by Tad Szulc and Jack Anderson in the fall of 1974, saying that Option 2 was never chosen and that no decision was reached to change policy in accordance with Option 2. Technically, these statements may be correct, but they are in fact completely misleading.

Kissinger recommended to President Nixon in January, 1970, that he approve a general posture of partial relaxation along the lines of Option 2 as presented at the National Security Council meeting on December 10, 1969. This would mean, he wrote, balancing US relations in the area by compensating for, rather than abandoning, US tangible interests in the white states, lowering the anti-apartheid profile at the United Nations, quietly relaxing bilateral relations with South Africa by taking a less doctrinaire approach to mutual problems, avoiding pressure on the Portuguese and increasing aid (by about $5 million) and making other gestures to black states.

Option 2 was not adopted verbatim, true. Certain of its features given as operational examples were altered. Kissinger recommended that through 1970 at least the Navy continue to limit calls at South African ports to emergencies only. Clearly, this sort of action remains too highly visible, invites racial antagonism in the crew and is a politically volatile issue without any compensating necessity to require it. EXIM policies would be loosened some, but not all the way; the test seemingly was whether the loosening up amounted to a visible promotion of trade.

Subsequently, the decisions taken were, apparently, incorporated in a National Security Decision Memorandum, dated close to the end of January, 1970.

What Option 2 represents is a compromise, a straddle between

Option 1 — which was advocated by the Department of Defense and is often called the Dean Acheson position, after its advocate over the years — and Option 3, which was a codification of the Kennedy-Johnson-era policy advocated by the State Department's liberal Africa Bureau. These advocacies continue. Thus, the repeal of the Byrd Amendment, which undercut US compliance with UN sanctions against Rhodesia, is advocated professionally by the Africa Bureau, yet disparaged, discouraged or delayed by Defense, Treasury and Commerce, each for a different reason which is thoroughly "tangible": strategic, commercial and economic. The result is a kind of dichotomy, a hypocritical, rhetorical stance which is politically unenacted and a continuing stasis in which the White House remains unwilling to bend Republican arms lest it offend its business patrons to put marginal pressure on the Ian Smith regime. Meanwhile, however, the Africa Bureau is gradually being weeded out. The liberals are being rusticated. Donald Easum, former Assistant Secretary for African Affairs, for example, has been removed and sent to Nigeria, having returned from a tour of Africa during which he spoke in forceful terms against South Africa's intransigence. Foreign policy officers with experience in key countries of Latin America where CIA operations have been executed (such as Chile, Guatemala and Cuba) have been installed in South Africa, Zaire and elsewhere. These changes have not all been effective. Nathaniel Davis, for example, a veteran of Chile, opposed Kissinger's hardline policy on Angola, even though he had been appointed to succeed Easum (apparently because he was believed to be much more sensitive to Kissinger's wishes than Easum).

Within the dialectical process, however, the synthesis of contradictory tendencies was achieved by the application of a Kissingerian analysis. By reading NSSM 39, we are allowed to see how the staff approached a problem by laying it out in its full factual detail with all US underlying interests bared. What is so chilling is the rationality of what is so fundamentally wrong and morally desiccated. Here we see realpolitik at work in the nude, unclothed with diplomatic rhetoric and unadorned by obfuscation. Here we can see the balancing of interests, the trade-offs and the considerations that preoccupy *the* national security manager of our time, who has shaped US foreign policy for seven years, almost single-handedly.

I agree fully with the admirable analysis of the authors' introduction to NSSM 39, which needs no further elaboration. Perhaps it may not be amiss to stress a few points which deserve special emphasis:

First, the writers of the classified document do not seem to understand what black people want when they say they want majority rule. The issue is defined as the "racial issue" or "discrimination". At no point is it defined as a transfer of power to Africans. The most that the NSSM writers could envision the United States working for would be "progress" involving "participation" by blacks in a white power structure, a qualified franchise, advances in wages and organizational power, etc. Such progress clearly does not amount to majority rule; in fact this sort of proposal is similar to the proposal rejected recently by the moderate leader of the Zimbabwe African National Council (internal wing), Joshua Nkomo.

Second, we should understand the new significance of a minerals shortage which has been illuminated and studied since the Arab oil embargo. South Africa and Rhodesia are now more important to the survival of the industrialized western world than ever before. Specifically, I would like to refer to the declassified version of a White House study of 16 strategic minerals, which was published in December 1974*:

> Embargoes of raw materials are highly unlikely. They do not make economic sense in terms of producers' revenue objectives . . . . An embargo, however, may be undertaken for political reasons, as in the case of the Arab oil producers . . . .
> Canada, Australia, or South Africa would be unlikely to participate in any embargo of exports to the United States, Western Europe or Japan. Since these three countries are the most important sources of raw materials for the United States (and are very important for Western Europe and Japan), any embargo threat for commodities they produce is greatly diminished.

If Western Europe proceeds with its projected plans to shift its energy sources to nuclear power, there will be a very significant shortage of nuclear fuel by 1980 unless new enrichment facilities are brought into existence close to sources of uranium. South Africa has 30 percent of the world's uranium reserves and a new uranium enrichment process.

Third, the United States intervention in Angola meant that the United States began to assume active responsibility for securing the stability of the southern African region against liberation movements that are anti-imperialist. Through the CIA, the US assisted in bringing about the active collaboration of South Africa with Zambia, Zaire and two black political movements in a common plan of action. That it failed does not mean that similar kinds of operations will not be attempted utilizing the lessons of that experience. It is interesting to note in the NSSM 39 the emphasis the authors place on South Africa and Zambia as key elements in the plan to stabilize the region.

I am personally very grateful that the publisher of this American edition has had the courage and the foresight to put into the hands of

---

* Special Report, *Critical Imported Materials*, Washington, D.C. Council on International Economic Policy, December, 1974.

ordinary citizens the plain facts about how "our" security is planned through collaboration with racist and fascist regimes. That knowledge should arm us to resist.

EDGAR LOCKWOOD
Washington, DC
April 9, 1976

PART I

National Security
Study Memorandum 39
in Perspective

MOHAMED A. EL-KHAWAS AND BARRY COHEN

INTRODUCTION

Recent revelations of covert operations of the Central Intelligence Agency, including plots to assassinate foreign leaders, raise difficult questions about the conduct of United States foreign policy. The *Village Voice* publication of the Presidentially-censored House Report on the CIA has brought to light some terrifying facts about intelligence activities in Africa and elsewhere, demonstrating the considerable discrepancy between public policy pronouncements and action.

The CIA report is not the only classified document on foreign policy to find its way to the public. The Nixon and Ford administrations have been known for their selective leakage of information to the American people. Henry A. Kissinger has made widespread use of this convenient mechanism, leaking bits and pieces of documents to a selected group of reporters, legislators and academicians whenever he wanted to tilt public opinion in a certain direction.

During the early seventies, National Security Study Memorandum 39 (1969) was partially quoted by a handful of people – a situation which aroused considerable curiosity about the content of the total document. NSSM 39 is a background study of relations between the United States and southern Africa that was prepared to demarcate various policy options for the Republican administration. The role played by NSSM 39 in shaping US policy toward southern Africa since 1970 is the subject of ongoing controversy. On the one hand, in 1975, Donald B. Easum, later the Assistant Secretary of State for African Affairs, emphatically denied that any of the proposed policy options in NSSM 39 were included in the final policy initiated by the Republican administration.[1] On the other hand, several critics of US-African policy, including Goler T. Butcher, Willard Johnson and Congressman Charles C. Diggs, believe that Nixon's policy was indeed based not only on NSSM 39 in general but also, more specifically, on Option 2 as outlined in the document. Donald E. McHenry commented that "We have seen a coincidence between the recommendations contained in that study and United States actions."[2]

If the confusion created by disclosure of only certain portions of the document is to be cleared up, the complete and unabridged text of NSSM 39 must be made available to everyone. This book is intended to provide a framework whereby the reader can check current policy pronouncements and actions in relation to southern Africa against the views expressed in the document. Careful reading of NSSM 39 will contribute to a better understanding of the controversy surrounding the nature and direction of Nixon-Ford foreign policy toward Africa.

The remainder of this introduction presents, first, an overview of NSSM 39, emphasizing its general content and historical significance. Second, Nixon's policy toward southern Africa is analyzed in detail with frequent comparisons between recommendations in the document and specific policy actions. Finally, Ford's policy toward southern Africa is examined in an attempt to determine whether or not Richard M. Nixon's abrupt departure from office résulted in any major policy changes.

OVERVIEW

In 1975, United States policy toward southern Africa was challenged by some Senators and Congressmen who feared that covert military support for one faction in the Angolan civil war might lead to a Vietnam-type entanglement and to an uncomfortably close synchronization between American efforts and South Africa's first military intervention in a black-ruled nation. This fear — along with growing evidence that the professed American commitment to national self-determination has occasionally been sacrificed in favor of certain obscure but nonetheless powerful strategic and economic interests in the white-ruled countries of Africa — has triggered a demand by the Black Congressional Caucus and liberal politicans that US-African policy be scrutinized more closely. Repeated attempts to investigate this policy have, however, been hampered by the lack of adequate data and the failure of the Republican administration to disclose the real reasons behind its policy actions.

Critics have charged that the United States has no coherent African policy, that decisions relating to southern Africa are made on an ad hoc basis in an attempt to strike a balance between the conflicting and irreconcilable objectives of African and white-minority-ruled states. The US has tried to pacify the growing number of African governments who look upon the US relationship with colonial and settler regimes in southern Africa as "tacit acceptance of racism;"[3] at the same time the American government has tried to avoid seriously incommoding Pretoria and Lisbon — governments with whom the US has common economic and strategic interests. The Kennedy-Johnson administration was criticized for its failure to translate its public denouncements of apartheid and colonialism in Africa into actions that might have forced colonial and minority regimes to alter their policies. Southern Africa ranked low among the nation's priorities as the Johnson administration became more and more involved in the Vietnam war. In short, the United States showed no serious concern over finding solutions to these African problems; Washington was content to remain aloof as long as the Soviet Union and China made no sudden moves to alter the black-white imbalance of power in the area.

The inauguration of President Nixon brought hope that the administration would take a fresh look at US-African policy since it was the new President's prerogative to extend or discontinue the policy of the previous administration. As it turned out, Nixon, like Ford after him, chose to rely on the advice of Henry Kissinger, first as national security advisor and later as Secretary of State. Despite his critical influence on the direction and substance of American foreign policy throughout the Nixon and Ford administrations, Kissinger's views on southern Africa have been obscure and ambiguous. Some argue that the chief reason Kissinger paid so little attention to southern African issues prior to the Angolan civil war was that he had to deal with urgent problems more directly pertinent to the US national interest. Others maintain that, in contrast to his thorough knowledgeability about European affairs, his knowledge of Africa is scant.[4]

To understand recent US policy toward southern Africa, then, it is necessary to zero in on Kissinger, who has become the architect of American foreign policy. Most notably, as the President's assistant for national security affairs, he strengthened the role of the White House, thereby advancing his plan for centralizing and maintaining the secrecy of crucial foreign-policy decisions. This process is consistent with the views expressed in "Bureaucracy, Politics and Strategy" (1968), in which he stated:

> The position the political leader takes is much influenced by the type of intellectual that sometimes quite accidentally winds up in his entourage . . . . Some of the key decisions are kept to a very small circle while the bureaucracy happily continues working away in ignorance of the fact that decisions are being made.[5]

National Security Study Memorandum 39 (1969) is valuable for understanding both US policy toward southern Africa and Kissinger's role in shaping it.

In 1969, under the direction and guidance of Kissinger, the National Security Council Interdepartmental Group for Africa — consisting of representatives of the Central Intelligence Agency and of the Departments of State and Defense — prepared a comprehensive review of US-southern Africa policy. They were assisted by other departments and agencies including Treasury, Commerce, the Joint Chiefs of Staff, the Agency for International Development and the National Aeronautical and Space Administration. The study review was intended to provide the National Security Council (NSC) with an analysis of "(1) the background and future prospects of major problems in the area; (2) alternative views of the US interest in southern Africa; and (3) the full range of basic strategies and policy options open to the US."[6] It is important to note that the report did not recommend any specific policy option but rather merely listed alternatives, leaving it to the NSC to consider these alternatives and make the final selection.

To some observers, the significance of NSSM 39 "lies in the glimpse it affords of Kissinger's realpolitik analysis, unadorned by rhetoric and devoid of charisma."[7] In addition, it gives a detailed picture of how decisions are deliberated within the highest policy-making circles in Washington. Finally, it reflects some of the ambivalence of American foreign policy that was kept secret under the Nixon administration.

NSSM 39 provides rare insights on the Nixon-Kissinger stance on the liberation struggle in southern Africa. Up to this point, only a modest amount of information has been available on the Nixon administration's involvement in southern Africa, and even the presumably factual material appearing in various publications presents widely conflicting claims and information. Further, because the US role has been so controversial, most of the published analysis on US policy has been highly polemical in nature.

In preparing NSSM 39, the NSC staff diligently sifted the information then available in an attempt to construct a comprehensive picture out of fragmented pieces. The historical significance of the document lies in its detailed examination of the American interest in, and policy toward, each country in the southern African region — including arguments both for and against continuing the policies of Kennedy and Johnson — and in the many important interpretative statements made by the NSC staff.

As a source of factual data, NSSM 39 also contributes substantially to our understanding of US policy toward southern Africa. Particularly useful, if somewhat dated, are the ten annexes to the document, which contain facts and figures on African countries and on American activities in the area, all of which were provided by the US agencies in charge of such functions. For example, the US department of Commerce provided statistical information on US direct investment in and trade with Africa. These figures constitute a basis for determining any given country's economic importance to the United States. In addition, they enable us to assess the monetary value of the American economic relationship with the white minority regimes vis-a-vis the rest of Africa. The report leaves no doubt that, with the possible exception of Zambia, US interests in black-ruled countries of southern Africa — whether measured in absolute or relative terms — are limited. In contrast, the US has valuable economic, defense and scientific interests in the white regimes, particularly South Africa.

Another important annex is the Agency for International Development report on the tactical and strategic uses of American aid to promote US interests in the region. Stripped of the familiar rhetoric which characterizes most government pronouncements on aid policy, this discussion permits the reader to appreciate the mode of determining the direction and quantity of aid in terms of the donor's politico-economic goals.

The assessment of Congressional reaction to US policy on southern Africa, in Annex 6, notes that many of the Congressmen and Senators who take an interest in Africa have stressed the link between racial conditions in South Africa and civil rights efforts in the US. Increasing recognition of this link could lead to important developments among various American black organizations as they grow progressively more aware of the struggles against oppression in southern Africa. On the other hand, the report also mentions that a small group in Congress, mainly from the South, has favored closer relations with the white minority governments.

The text of NSSM 39 opens with a brief review of US interests and policy in southern Africa, emphasizing specific measures initiated inside and outside the United Nations by previous administrations in response to the eruption of the national liberation struggle in southern Africa, a struggle directed primarily against colonial and white minority regimes. It notes that, although the US denounced apartheid and imposed a ban on the sale of ammunition and military equipment to South Africa, it consistently refused to restrict American trade and investment or to reduce the scientific collaboration (on nuclear research projects, among other things) that was taking place in South Africa. On the other hand, the US has consistently taken a pro-African stance on the question of Namibia (South West Africa) and joined the majority of the UN General Assembly in voting for the termination of the South African mandate. Further, when the Rhodesian problem arose, the Johnson administration reaffirmed its basic commitment to the principles of self-determination and human rights but, at the same time, generally deferred to the British strategy, withholding recognition of the Ian Smith regime and imposing economic sanctions against Rhodesia.

Next, NSSM 39 compares the US policy toward southern Africa with British and French policy in an attempt to show that the US government took more steps against white minority regimes than did either Britain or France; indeed, the latter ignored the UN arms embargo against South Africa. At the same time, the document reveals that in formulating its southern African policy the US, as the leading Western power, could not ignore certain global realities. Among the real-world considerations affecting US policy toward southern Africa were:

- the strategic importance of southern Africa, particularly with the closing of the Suez Canal following the 1967 Middle East war and the increased Soviet naval activities in the Indian Ocean;

- the US need to use overflight and landing facilities for military aircraft heading to and from Indochina;

- significant investment and balance of trade advantages to both Britain and the US in South Africa;

- South Africa's status as the major gold supplier in the capitalist world and its importance in guaranteeing the useful operation of the two-tier gold price system.[8]

Interestingly, NSSM 39 highlights the dilemma arising out of the US desire to reconcile conflicting interests in the area: It was feared that maintaining close ties with the colonial and settler regimes in southern Africa might, in the long run, jeopardize American relations with the rest of Africa and other Third World countries. Therefore, US policy attempted "to balance its economic, scientific, and strategic interests in the white states with the political interest of disassociating the US from the white regimes and their repressive racial policies."[9]

It is not easy to formulate a policy along these lines; instead, American policy-makers made ad hoc decisions after assessing the political cost or advantages of a particular action. One consequence of the absence of a definitive policy was that some policy matters were shelved or indefinitely postponed.

To keep the problem in perspective, however, the NSC staff thought it necessary to spell out as succinctly as possible the objectives of US policy in southern Africa. This is the first instance where American objectives in the region, as outlined by government policy-planners, appear in print. The objectives are stated as follows:

- to improve the US standing in black Africa and internationally on the racial issue

- to minimize the likelihood of escalation of violence in the area and risk of US involvement

- to minimize the opportunities for the USSR and Communist China to exploit the racial issue in the region for propaganda

advantage and to gain political influence with black governments and liberation movements

- to encourage moderation of the current rigid racial and colonial
policies of the white regimes

- to protect economic, scientific, and strategic interests and opportunities in the region, including the orderly marketing of South
Africa's gold production.[10]

The NSC staff acknowledged that some of these objectives were conflicting and irreconcilable.

To arrive at policy recommendations, the NSC staff decided to
demarcate the areas of agreement and controversy within government
circles. They agreed that American interests in the area, though economically and politically important, were not vital to US security.[11] The
US was nevertheless interested in encouraging the conflicting parties to
solve the racial problems of southern Africa, because they had become
major issues with international repercussions. The US was worried about
the growing influence of the Soviet Union and China in the area and the
possibility of American-Soviet confrontation if the problem became
acute.

The areas of significant disagreement within the American bureaucracy concerned the prospect for peaceful changes in southern Africa
and the effectiveness of external pressure in causing white minority
governments to modify their racist policies. There was also no consent
on the extent to which close ties with South Africa and Portugal could
damage US interests in the rest of Africa and elsewhere.

The NSC staff examined current US policy, which insisted that
"consultation (was) preferable to confrontation."[12] Previous administrations had taken a firm view that force was not an appropriate vehicle
for bringing about constructive change; they had resisted the attempt to
impose punitive economic measures against South Africa on the grounds
that such measures (a) might require American military involvement for
their implementation, (b) were likely to be ineffective because South
Africa's major trading partners were unlikely to impose economic
sanctions against the Pretoria government and (c) might result in
hardening the positions of the colonial and settler regimes, thereby
closing the door to any possible compromise.

With all these variables in mind, the NSC staff proceeded to sort
policy alternatives for the Nixon administration, arriving at five options
that were broad in nature and often in conflict with each other. After
stating a premise for each option, the staff outlined the general policy
posture, illustrated by some operational examples, and concluded with

a list of the pros and cons of adopting that particular option. One must not expect to find in NSSM 39 a detailed description of "the types of action which would be consistent with the option's thrust," since the authors never intended to write "a specific scenario for operational action."[13] They were satisfied with simply mentioning a few examples to clarify the policy position under consideration.

Although the NSC staff did not endorse any specific policy option, the more detailed rationale and fuller outline given to Option 2 suggests that they were inclined to favor it. Since Option 3 was merely a continuation of the policies inherited from two previous Democratic administrations, it was doubtful that the Nixon administration would choose it. Criticized by some American conservatives for "its precarious combination of moralistic public rhetoric and limited quiet diplomatic entreaty,"[14] Option 3 was widely regarded by both Africans and whites as "expedient and hypocritical."[15] Options 1, 4 and 5 — calling for either total disengagement or total US backing of one party in the conflict — could never seriously have been considered as policy alternatives in view of the US economic, scientific and strategic interests at stake. These options were meaningless, because big-power politics were already at play. The Soviet Union and China were giving material and diplomatic support to the liberation movements and exploiting African racial and colonial conflicts to their political advantage. Moreover, liberal and black leaders in the US had without success urged previous administrations to stop doing business with minority regimes in southern Africa. It is inconceivable that the Nixon administration — which had the backing of industrialists, southern Democrats and northern conservatives — would seriously consider either becoming neutral or siding with the liberation movements; to do so might put an end to the highly profitable American investment and trade in South Africa and Angola as well as cutting off US access to rare minerals and to the Indian Ocean and the Azores.

What finally becomes glaringly obvious in NSSM 39 is the complete lack of concern over the aspirations and fate of the African people. The document makes it clear that the US had no genuine interest in solving racial and colonial conflicts in southern Africa; American involvement in the area was not a matter of choice on the part of Washington but of necessity created by the worldwide attention given to these problems. The US became involved not out of commitment to fundamental human rights and basic democratic principles but "because other countries have made it so."[16]

In retrospect, Nixon's southern African policy can be seen as derived from a false premise: that minority regimes were "tough, determined and increasingly self-confident,"[17] capable of holding out indefinitely. NSSM 39, therefore, dismissed the possibility of basic changes in the power structure in southern Africa. It failed to anticipate the coup d'etat in Lisbon, which triggered a chain of events in southern Africa that eventually resulted in an altered balance of power between Africans and whites. On the basis of this false premise, the US was willing "to accept political arrangements short of guaranteed progress toward majority rule," provided that some assurances be given for "[broader] political participation in some form by the whole population."[18]

Although "stability" very profitably serves the interests of US corporations, the impact of the exploitative colonial and apartheid systems on the lives of Africans did not fall within the NSC's "framework of analysis." Armed revolutionary struggle was perceived as a destabilizing factor which could serve the interests of only China or the Soviet Union. This inability to comprehend the dynamic of the liberation movements is significant. In the Nixon-Kissinger scheme for restructuring the international system, revolutionary states such as China are accorded "legitimacy." African revolutionary movements, on the other hand, must be contained and defeated. This distinction is evidenced in the document's analysis of the liberation struggle in southern Africa. The NSC staff found it sufficient to summarize the history of each southern African liberation movement, assessing its strength, the source of its financial and military assistance, its sanctuaries and the areas of its guerrilla activities inside any given country. None of this information sheds new light on the intensity of the struggle for self-government and independence; rather, it serves mainly as a review of the available information on the subject.

The NSSM 39 approach to formulating foreign policy is inherently weak, because there is no way of predicting future developments without the possibility of error. Though the policy resulting from such an approach may protect short-term US interests, it can well prove harmful in the long run. For instance, the coolness in US-Mozambican relations can come as no surprise; it is largely a natural reaction by FRELIMO to the military and economic assistance that successive US administrations rendered to the Portuguese during the long years of the liberation struggle. Donald F. McHenry comments that such a policy approach "quickly becomes a Christmas-tree-type listing of specific relations with the areas in which so-called 'tangible interests' appear more important than 'intangible interests,' even though those 'tangible interests' are not 'essential' and are relatively minor in terms of overall United States relations."[19]

NIXON POLICY TOWARD SOUTHERN AFRICA

The main outlines of the Nixon-Kissinger policy toward southern Africa were laid down after the completion of NSSM 39. On December 9, 1969, Kissinger discussed with the NSC the various policy options presented in the study, advising that the US choose a policy which would in no way threaten its national interests in that part of the world.

Because of the overriding preoccupation with Vietnam, along with increasing domestic pressure to end the Indochina war, the Nixon administration favored maintaining the status quo in southern Africa to whatever extent possible. The deliberations of the President, guided by Kissinger, led to the acceptance of Option 2 as the basis for Nixon's policy toward that troubled region. This policy, which implied a minimum initiative in southern Africa, seemed to line up the US on the side of the white minority regimes.

This policy choice was in keeping with Kissinger's view that, because of their growing reliance on the Soviet Union, Cuba and China for material assistance, most nationalist liberation movements were "communist stooges" and, if successful in wresting power from a colonial regime, would inevitably pursue an anti-Western policy. Kissinger deeply distrusted revolutionary groups, considering them a threat to his design for international tranquility, which depended upon stable relations among the big powers.[20] His policy recommendation derived from three NSSM assumptions: "(1) if violence in the area escalates, US interests will increasingly be threatened;[21] . . . (2) the whites are here to stay and the only way that constructive change can come about is through them ; . . . (3) there is no hope for the blacks to gain the political rights they seek through violence, which will only lead to chaos and increased opportunities for the communists."[22]

Thus, Kissinger's policy rested not on moral considerations nor on concern for human rights and fundamental democratic principles but instead on practical considerations; it represented a response to the American experience with the wars of national liberation in Vietnam. His immediate concern was to prevent an open war in southern Africa, a war which might drag in the US just at the time when the Nixon administration had its hands full in Indochina. Kissinger wanted to set up the general framework for Nixon's southern African policy and then turn it over to the powerless State Department to handle, with instructions to minimize the use of violence and to encourage peaceful change. The result was a total indifference, on the part of the US, to African aspirations for majority rule and an obvious tilt toward minority regimes.

The Nixon policy tended to follow Option 2 of the NSSM 39. It was decided to maintain "public opposition" to colonial and racial policies in southern Africa but to pursue a quiet policy which would "relax political and economic restrictions on the white states."[23] The desire was to "increase communication and selective involvement" with colonial and settler regimes on the theory that friendly persuasion would be more likely than would condemnation to bring about changes in their policies and racial practices.[24] It was hoped that the US involvement in southern Africa could be kept at a low profile. As Kissinger put it:

> We have as a country to ask ourselves the question of whether it should be the principal goal of American foreign policy to transform the domestic structure of societies with which we deal or whether the principal exercise of our foreign policy should be toward affecting the foreign policy of those societies.[25]

This line of thinking is consistent with his view that "foreign policy is essentially global strategy and . . . domestic considerations and pressures should not be allowed to impinge on it."[26] It overlooks, however, the fact that US policy has not always followed such distinctions. The revelations about the US role in the overthrow of Allende in Chile provide a recent example.[27]

The heavy US involvement in Vietnam had profound influence on Nixon's response to southern Africa. The enormous outlays of money, equipment and personnel for the Indochina war left little time, energy or money for other problems; further, when other issues did demand attention, militaristic or strategic considerations predominated. The Nixon administration could not extricate itself from the overriding preoccupation with Vietnam or from the growing domestic political pressures inherited from its predecessor. In addition, Nixon had undoubtedly been encouraged by his political backers, many of whom had business interests — industrial and banking — in southern Africa, to take a conservative stance.[28]

In accordance with this new policy, American officials were told to cut down their criticism of minority regimes and to keep the lid on racial and colonial conflicts in southern Africa. These instructions, issued in January, 1970, marked the beginning of the new Nixon-Kissinger "policy of communication" and a departure from the Kennedy-Johnson policies, which had been designed to maintain some kind of credibility with African leaders. The Nixon-Kissinger policy was aimed at establishing bridges with white minority regimes through "selective relaxation" and with border African states through a modest aid program ($5 million) that would encourage them to modify their policies. It was hoped that this approach would put the US in a position to bring the two groups together and pressure them into moderation and nonviolent change.[29] Such a policy would allow for some modification of the status quo by giving representation to the black majority without endangering white dominance. It would result in increased contact with minority regimes at the cost of decreased access to African diplomats and leaders. The State Department and other agencies were handed the task of implementing this uneven diplomacy, leaving Kissinger free to deal with more pressing problems (e.g., the Vietnam war, East-West relations, China) that impinged more directly on US interests and national security. This policy would remain unchanged so long as the Soviet Union and China made no attempt to extend their spheres of influence in southern Africa — a move that would not be tolerated by the Nixon administration. Nixon's policy was designed to localize racial and colonial conflicts in the region with minimal foreign intervention and to encourage white and African leaders to compromise and negotiate toward a solution. It represented a rejection of the concept of "one man, one vote," and its consequence was a slow but steady shift toward minority regimes.

At this point, to elucidate more fully the broad outlines of the new policy as embodied in NSSM 39 and to determine how closely actual policy has conformed with the approach of Option 2, it is necessary to examine Nixon-Kissinger policy toward each country in the southern African region.

South Africa

Although NSSM 39 was intended to cover the entire region of southern Africa, its attention was concentrated primarily on US interests in South Africa, an emphasis which suggests that South Africa was the cornerstone of US southern African policy. The study not only accepted Pretoria's central role in shaping the destiny of southern Africa but apparently also considered it a reliable ally, indispensable to Western interests.

The study argued that Western interests were best served by a policy of open communcation with white minority regimes carried out at "an acceptable political price."[30] In reaching this conclusion and thus rationalizing the policy tilt in favor of the white minority regimes, NSSM 39 cited the following considerations. First, because of its growing dependency on African labor, Pretoria would soon be forced to develop more acceptable racial policies. Second, the US was not forced to take an active role since there was no immediate challenge to Pretoria's power: South Africa was judged to be militarily and economically strong and fully capable of avoiding or moderating any potential violence within its borders. In addition, Africans and black Americans were too preoccupied with their own internal problems to oppose vigorously the policy of communication.[31]

The Nixon administration apparently accepted these arguments and decided to proceed with the new policy, whose object was to encourage orderly and evolutionary change in South Africa. The Nixon administration used the news column of Ken Owen, Washington-based representative of South Africa's Argus news chain, as one vehicle for relaying this new policy stance to Pretoria. Beginning in 1970, his column reflected the clear message that the Republican administration wanted to improve relations with South Africa.[32] Other evidence of a shift in policy abounded. The administration failed to criticize Pretoria, for instance, when it refused to grant a visa to black American tennis player Arthur Ashe. Furthermore, South Africa's ambassador was granted direct access to Kissinger, and its officials were warmly received by the White House and the Department of Defense. These meetings, largely unannounced and little publicized, were often held without the prior knowledge of the State Department and even over its objections. It seems that the State Department was intentionally kept in the dark about these high-level meetings so that critics of the new Nixon policy would be misled by the continuing State Department denunciations of apartheid.

Later, when Kissinger became the Secretary of State, he chose to overrule Africa Bureau recommendations to deny private visits by South African officials. In January, 1974, Kissinger permitted a US visit by Pretoria's Minister of Information, Cornelius Mulder, over the direct objection of the Bureau. Mulder met with Vice President Gerald Ford and such senior Pentagon officials as Vice Admiral Ray Peet, who was in charge of international security affairs and the Indian Ocean. In May, Admiral Hugo Biermann, the Chief of the South African Defense Forces, held meetings in the Pentagon with Admiral Thomas Moorer, Chairman of the US Joint Chiefs of Staff, and with J. W. Middendorf, Acting Secretary of the Navy.[33]

The US stance in the United Nations also became more sympathetic to South Africa. Previously, US votes on colonial issues at the UN had frequently been abstentions. However, under Nixon, "the balance of US voting . . . tipped to the negative."[34] In 1972, the US voted negatively on seven major resolutions on southern Africa and colonial issues and abstained on one other resolution. The US stance on these votes was generally in consonance with that of South Africa and Portugal.

As Ken Owen commented in the *Johannesburg Star* in January, 1974, "The Democratic administration's drift towards a policy of isolating South Africa has been checked and, in marginal areas where it was politically feasible, reversed."[35] While overstating the difference, Owen's observations nevertheless reflected Pretoria's pleasure, usually muted, with the Nixon Administration's approach to the region.

US Business Involvement in South Africa

Nixon's policy followed the emphasis of NSSM 39, which had placed far greater weight on American economic and military interests than on the merits of political issues in South Africa and Namibia. Like his predecessors, he continued to oppose any coercive measures against South Africa and refused to comply with UN resolutions calling for sanctions. The Nixon administration, with the high value it placed on American investment and trade with Pretoria, considered curbs on business activities to be unthinkable.

During the Nixon years, US investment in South Africa (and to a much lesser degree in Namibia) expanded substantially. Although its official policy was to "neither encourage nor discourage investment,"[36] the administration made available certain facilities of the Export-Import Bank and gave government-supported loans or guarantees for investment in South Africa. In addition, the Commerce Department supplied information and other services to US firms considering investment in South Africa. More importantly, in a reversal of policy dating back to 1964, the Nixon administration in 1972 authorized the Export-Import Bank to guarantee a ten-year loan of $48.6 million to South Africa for the purchase of diesel locomotives. The loan guarantee was based on a March, 1971, decision that removed a former restriction on the bank's loans to five-year terms.[37]

The volume of US investment showed marked growth between 1968 and 1973. Total investment increased from $692 million to $1.2 billion, or by 73 percent in a five-year period.[38] This accelerated pace of economic investment moved the US to second place among foreign investors, with approximately 15 percent of total foreign investment in South Africa.

US trade with South Africa also increased during the Nixon era. Exports to South Africa increased from $450 million in 1968 to $746 million in 1973, and imports from South Africa increased from $250 million to $377 million during the same period.[39] The net result was a very favorable balance of trade for the United States.

This increased level of investment and trade with South Africa was of substantial benefit to US economic interests. The favorable balance of trade was particularly important in view of continuing US deficits in its international balance of payments and its troubles with economic recession at home. The favorable investment terms were attractive, too: largely because of cheap African labor, the annual rate of return on direct American investment in South Africa has been 17 or 19 percent since 1968.[40]

The differing trade needs of the two countries were also compatible. The US sold industrial goods to South Africa — mainly machinery, vehicles, aircraft, chemicals and electrical equipment — that significantly benefited South Africa's economic expansion in such critical areas as computer technology, heavy capital goods, oil exploration and chemical industries. In turn, the US imported crucial minerals, such as platinum, chromium and gold, from Pretoria. The US has an especially critical interest in maintaining a stable supply of gold from South Africa, which has been the major gold supplier to the non-communist world. As former Assistant Secretary of State Donald Easum has remarked, the US "has a collateral interest in the contribution that orderly marketing of South African gold makes to the world financial system."[41]

Undoubtedly, the Nixon administration was under a great deal of pressure to encourage US exports and to facilitate American investment in South Africa. US corporations with investments there held strong views on the matter and vigorously opposed any governmental action to cut down on their investment.* In all, more than 350 American firms were engaged in business in South Africa. They formed a strong lobby that was active in persuading policy-makers against any kind of economic disengagement.[42] US arms manufacturers lobbied to lift the arms embargo, for instance, because they were losing some of their South African market to France, which had continued the sale of arms to Pretoria. They argued that the arms sales should be viewed primarily as business transactions, that would greatly help ease the growing US deficit in its balance of payments.

---

* Although often overlooked, the US involvement in Namibia (South West Africa) deserves some attention. In an uncharacteristic action, the Nixon administration in 1970 announced that it would officially discourage investment in Namibia. To demonstrate its sincerity, it would no longer make Export-Import Bank credit guarantees available for trade with Namibia. Furthermore, US investment that had been implemented there after the Security Council Resolution 2145 (1966) would not obtain US government insurance against any claims of a future lawful Namibia.

Many US firms, employing the advantages of the multinational corporation, marketed their products in Namibia through South African subsidiaries. According to the most recent study on foreign capital in Namibia, the value of US investment in 1971 amounted to \$45 million. As the authors of the report state: "Despite the official steps to discourage US companies from extending their investment in Namibia . . . American investment — in common with British, West German, French and Canadian — is still increasing. Although these figures look comparatively small, within the context of the Namibian economy they are very large indeed." Roger Murray and others, *The Role of Foreign Firms in Namibia.* London: African Publications Trust, 1974. See also Reed Kramer and Tami Hultman, *A Profile of United States Contribution to Underdevelopment in Namibia.* New York: Corporate Information Center, April 1973; Winifred Courtney and Jennifer Davis, *Namibia: United States Corporate Involvement.* New York: The Africa Fund, March 1972.

For many years, US corporations responded to critics of apartheid with the argument that their presence in South Africa provided a moderating influence on the economic system. Because of the limited size of the white labor force and the substantial demand for skilled workers created by American investment, they argued, the inexorable laws of economic expansion would compel Pretoria to lower existing job barriers to Africans. Furthermore, American firms could help directly by improving the conditions of the African working force and by giving them greater economic power.

The Nixon administration took several actions that reflected acceptance of this argument. The State Department, for instance, continually encouraged US corporations to implement fair employment practices including better wages, training and fringe benefits for nonwhite labor. In February, 1973, it publicized some examples of good practices introduced by American firms. In summer, 1974, it urged American companies to enter into collective bargaining with African trade unions, even though they had not yet been recognized by South Africa.[43]

South Africa's black leadership sharply disagreed with this approach. On the contrary, they maintained that 15 years of substantial foreign investment in South Africa had been accompanied by expansion in the coercive powers of the state and repressive action against all meaningful opposition. Both Gatsha Buthelezi, Chief Minister of the Kwazulu homeland, and Beyers Naude, Director of the South African Christian Institute, have argued that "attempts to increase the responsibility of employers and investors within the system will do nothing to produce the radical [re] distribution of wealth and power which are essential prerequisites of justice and peace."[44]

There is one area of analysis in the NSSM document which is dealt with in a surprising degree of brevity: the strategic importance of the raw materials in southern Africa and the extent of US dependence on them (see Table 1). Should the NSSM document be written today, it is most likely that supplies of natural resources would be more extensively analysed. Concern that the US is rapidly becoming more dependent on foreign sources for critical fuels and raw materials has markedly increased in the 1970s.[45]

It is in this area of resource scarcity that the economic and strategic value of southern Africa must be considered. In August, 1971, the African Affairs Advisory Council submitted a study, *Africa's Resources*, to the State Department. It initially pointed out that

> Africa contains a major proportion of the world's reserves of a few commodities important to US strategic or economic needs. In the future, the US will probably have to look to Africa for, among other products, its chromite, platinum group metals,

tantalite, petalite, gold, long-fibered amosite and crocidolite asbestos, natural industrial diamond stones and phosphate rock
(in 20-30 years).[46]

Excluding tantalite, industrial diamonds and phosphate rock, it reiterated that they "are found primarily in almost unique concentrations in
southern Africa." The study concluded that "the US may in the long
run have to turn more to southern Africa for its chromite"[47] and other
critical minerals. The US already depended primarily on South Africa
(in 1968-1969 figures) for 40 percent of its antimony, 38 percent of its
chrome ore and more than one-third of its platinum group metals, as
well as 85 percent of its uranium oxide imports. In regard to other
minerals such as manganese and vanadium, South Africa will probably
be the future source for the United States.[48]

Table 1

Production of Minerals in Southern Africa[1] as a Percentage of World
Production.

	1967	*1968*	*1969*
Gold	68.3	68.8	68.8
Gem diamonds	62.2	64.0	63.6
Industrial diamonds	54.4	52.9	64.3
Cobalt (contained)	55.9	57.0	56.7
Chromite	32.1	31.7	31.5
Vanadium[2] (ore and concen.)	31.1	25.9	29.4
Platinum group metals	26.4	25.5	28.4
Vermiculite	30.2	29.0	30.7
Antimony	21.5	27.3	27.9
Copper (ore and concen.)	23.4	21.8	22.0
Uranium[3] (contained)	17.9	17.1	17.0
Manganese[4] (ore)	12.8	13.9	14.4
Beryllium[5] (Beryl)	7.0	8.7	10.4

1. Includes South Africa, Namibia, Botswana, Lesotho, Swaziland, Rhodesia,
   Angola, Mozambique, Zambia, Zaire, and Malagasy Republic.
2. Namibia production is of lead vanadate concentrate. South African production
   is of vanadium pentoxide.
3. "Free world" production only.
4. Percentage of Mn. concentrate differs according to country.
5. 1967 figures for Rhodesia taken from US import data.

Source: *Minerals Yearbook*, 1968 and 1969, US Department of the Interior.

Implementation of the US Arms Embargo

President Nixon accepted the recommendation embodied in Option 2 of NSSM 39 which suggested that his administration should "enforce [the] arms embargo against South Africa but with liberal treatment of equipment which could serve either military or civilian purposes."[49] Beginning in 1970, he swiftly moved to implement his new policy. In January, 1970, he announced that his administration would continue to impose an arms embargo against South Africa. Before the end of the year, however, Kissinger revised the guidelines governing the embargo. He liberalized restrictions placed by previous Democratic administrations on handling applications for "gray area" export licenses. The new guidelines provided substantial relaxation of controls in three areas: (1) certain items were taken off the validated license list; (2) items still under validated licensing controls, such as aircraft, were made available for export; and (3) items from the munitions control category were transferred to the validated license list.[50] These guidelines were interpreted by some critics as a move toward a gradual erosion of the arms embargo which had been imposed by the Kennedy administration.

The new guidelines were criticized by several observers,[51] but the administration did not change its plans. Furthermore, in September, 1970, David Newsom, Assistant Secretary of State for African Affairs, announced that the US was ready to accept license applications for the sale of executive-type transport aircraft to South Africa's military.[52] This announcement, which was interpreted as dramatic evidence of the substantial relaxation in the terms of the US arms embargo, was more symbolic than real, however, since Pretoria never applied for the purchase of VIP jet planes.

Table 2 shows that Nixon sold $219 million in aircraft to South Africa during his first term in the White House. This was in contrast to a total of $93 million between 1965 and 1968. At the same time, however, Nixon authorized the sale of fewer planes (743) than the number sold by the Johnson administration (1,076). This change — increased expenditures but fewer aircraft — was due largely to higher prices, differing aircraft and better equipment. The US did not approve the sale of aircraft until Pretoria had agreed to use them exclusively for civilian purposes.

Liberal and black Americans sharply denounced the sale of aircraft to South Africa, arguing that the distinction between the civilian or military use of aircraft was unrealistic. Jennifer Davis, Director of the American Office on Africa, questioned the judgment of the Nixon policy-makers in approving the sale of several hundred aircraft to South Africa in view of Pretoria's "contingency legislation to enable the Government to commandeer all civil aircraft in the event of an emergency, and . . . [its] special facilities for converting civil aircraft to various military uses aimed at internal repression."[53]

Table 2

The Number and the Value of Aircraft
Sold to South Africa, 1965-1972

Year	Number	Value
1965	235	$ 34,548,530
1966	208	4,519,595
1967	333	23,438,380
1968	200	30,398,139
Total	**1,076**	**92,904,644**
1969	284	42,503,604
1970	180	25,627,562
1971	135	70,357,608
1972	144	80,485,712
Total	**743**	**218,974,486**

Source: Implementation of the US Arms Embargo. Hearings of the Subcommittee on Africa, House Committee on African Affairs, 93rd Congress, 1st Session, March 20, 22 and April 6, 1973.

The Nixon administration also provided South Africa with parts, repairs and other services related either to preexisting contracts by the Defense Department or to commercial contracts for C-130 transport planes sold to South Africa prior to 1963. As shown in Table 3, the value of these services totalled $11 million between 1968 and 1972, compared to $9 million in the previous four years.

US trade in communications equipment for South Africa also increased substantially between 1968 and 1972. For example, the sale of electrical navigational aids doubled and sales of communications equipment "not elsewhere classified" more than tripled during this period. These two categories represented approximately 75 percent of the South African purchases in communications equipment.

Table 3

C—130 AIRCRAFT/SAAF SUPPORT PROGRAM

I.   Licensed export of spare parts, associated ground equipment and technical data — by calendar year:

1963	$1,282,000
1964	2,070,646
1965	857,000
1966	1,346,000
1967	2,728,439
1968	3,880,091
1969	3,777,815
1970	2,752,175
1971	2,798,836
1972	1,677,185
1973 (through Apr. 4, 1973)	92,387

II.   Center Wing Repair Program (April 1970 — June 1971) program price, $3,472,000.

III. T—56 Engine Overhaul Program (engines to be imported into US for overhaul and re-exported upon completion).
      (1) Total of engine repair program:
          (a) 46 T—56 engines to be imported, $552,000
          (b) Replacement parts during overhaul (estimated), $1,066,602
      (2) Portion of total program in (1) achieved up to 4 April 1973:
          (a) 10 T—56 engines imported 1972, $720,000.
          (b) 12 T—56 engines imported 1973, $144,000.
          (c) 10 T—56 engines re-exported 1973, $351,870.

Source: *Ibid.*

US corporations were allowed to supply equipment that could be easily applied to military purposes. For example, "IBM supplied at least four computers to the South African Department of Defense, while ITT equipment and expert knowledge have been applied to the regime's communications systems. General Electric, through its South African subsidiary, supplies about 95 percent of the diesel locomotives for South African railways."[54] In addition, between 1967 and 1972, about $10 million worth of herbicides were sold to Pretoria, and a General Motors plant was built in South Africa, specifically designed to allow for conversion to military production.[55]

The maintenance of space tracking stations and close assistance to the South African nuclear energy program by the US Atomic Energy Commission are two important examples of the close scientific-military ties between the two states. As was pointed out in NSSM 39, the NASA station was "of primary importance to the space program. Although alternate facilities have been constructed for use if necessary, they do not afford equivalent support."[56]

In perspective, the weight of much evidence suggests that the Nixon administration did substantially relax the arms embargo against South Africa after the NSSM 39 was completed, particularly by making available new items in the "gray area" that had been forbidden previously. This change caused Nixon critics to suggest that the arms embargo be tightened again. "Without arguing whether the relaxation in the 'gray' areas brought South Africa significant equipment," they argued that "the very fact of relaxation carried a significant signal of comfort to the National regime."[57]

That President Nixon paid little attention to the criticism of his South Africa policy was partly due to the important role South Africa played in the Kissinger scheme to counter the Soviet threat in the Indian Ocean and to enhance the security of the Cape area. The seriousness of the Soviet presence in the Indian Ocean was particularly emphasized after the closing of the Suez Canal in 1967 and the consequent increase in oil tankers carrying 80 percent of Western oil around the Cape.

In order to exploit the new circumstances in the Indian Ocean, the South African government had been pressing for a regional maritime alliance with the West for a number of years.[58] According to the British Anti-Apartheid Organization, it found a receptive audience in NATO and US naval councils. In November, 1972, the NATO Council requested SACLANT (the Supreme Allied Command in the Atlantic) to devise plans for the "protection" of supply routes around the Cape.[59] It wasn't until May, 1974, however, that the NATO press secretary admitted that SACLANT had this secret authorization to develop contingency plans for the protection of the Cape route. He also revealed that

NATO planners were examining options to be applied not only in wartime but also in "crisis situations."[60]

Formalization of the NATO moves to extend its operations beyond its traditional limits occurred at the NATO Council of Ministers meeting in June, 1974, in Ottawa. Tad Szulc commented that this constituted "a carte blanche for NATO to become involved wherever it wishes. . . . The uncertainty is whether the United States and some of its allies, encouraged by the license issued in Ottawa, may choose to regard South Africa's internal security in the face of black pressures as a justification for direct air or naval support, using SACLANT's contingency planning."[61]

A key element in South Africa's military links with NATO is the highly sophisticated communication and surveillance center, Silvermine, just north of the Simonstown naval base. This complex system, known as Project Advocaat, is capable of covering 25 million square miles of ocean stretching from South American to Bangladesh. A dispatch by the *Wall Street Journal* quoted a South African naval officer who revealed that the system at Silvermine is linked to the US via the American naval communications center in Derry, Northern Ireland.[62] Photostats of documents leaked to the British Anti-Apartheid movement provide evidence that several NATO countries, including the US, sold military equipment for Project Advocaat. In fact, "28 pieces of US equipment were delivered to Pretoria for Project Advocaat."[63]

The extension of the communications facility on Diego Garcia also meant that the US was moving toward establishment of a permanent naval presence in the Indian Ocean and much closer cooperation with South Africa. In August, 1974, the US House of Representatives approved a $29 million appropriation to expand Diego Garcia into a base for naval vessels.[64] Although this action was condemned by most nations bordering on the Indian Ocean, the US was determined, in accordance with the Kissinger strategy, to add the base to its defense plans in order to counter the Soviet buildup in the region. As many observers predicted, the accelerated interest in Diego Garcia has drawn Pretoria deeper into the strategic orbit of the US.

RHODESIA (ZIMBABWE)

The Nixon policy-makers generally continued the low-profile approach to Rhodesia that had become so characteristic of the Johnson administration. This approach, reflected in President Nixon's decision to keep the US consulate open in Salisbury,[65] substantially conformed with the policy outlined in Option 2 of NSSM 39. Despite African demands for stronger American efforts toward ending minority rule in

Rhodesia, Nixon did not initiate any new measures aimed at finding solutions to the constitutional problem in Rhodesia. Like his predecessor, he refused to support African efforts in the UN to secure the use of force against Ian Smith. However, as a gesture of good will, the administration was willing to withdraw all consular officials from Salisbury. This was the only commitment that Secretary of State William Rogers made on Rhodesia during his African tour in February, 1970. Shortly after his return, Rogers did announce that the US would close its consulate in Salisbury — a measure that was taken in response to Smith's proclamation of a new constitution and the establishment of a republic on March 2, 1970. Some observers have argued that the timing was merely convenient and that mounting pressure from Britain and the UN Security Council had been the decisive factor rather than the African trip by Rogers.[66]

Nixon did continue the policy of non-recognition of the white minority regime in Rhodesia, but departed from his predecessor's policy of imposing sanctions against the Smith regime. He pursued Option 2's recommendation that "without openly taking a position undermining the UK and the UN on Rhodesia, we would be more flexible in our attitude toward the Smith regime."[67] Kissinger specifically advocated gradual relaxation of sanctions and, to implement this new policy, suggested to the President in January, 1970, that "[Departments of] State, Treasury and Commerce begin to formulate . . . alternative approaches concerning US participation in sanctions."[68] The main purpose was to initiate measures to soften enforcement of sanctions. This was seen as an accommodation to those who argued for support and cooperation with the Smith regime even at the cost of ignoring US obligations under the UN Charter. Annex 4 of the NSSM document acknowledged that "certain columnists, pressure groups, pro-Rhodesian and South African organizations, some domestic ferroalloy producers and certain members of Congress [were] urging that the importation of Rhodesian chrome be permitted."[69]

The Nixon administration approved the 1971 legislation specifically allowing an exception for the importation of Rhodesian chrome — a measure which halted the ban that had been in effect since 1967. In doing so, the US became "the only country in the world that has passed a law requiring violation of [UN] sanctions against Rhodesia."[70] The Johnson administration had freely voted for and supported the sanctions in the Security Council and, therefore, the US was duty-bound to follow them.[71]

Critics of the administration felt that the lifting of the embargo could be interpreted as a "victory for racism and reaction"[72] and would place the US in company with South Africa and Portugal, both of which had openly ignored the UN sanctions and continued their business transactions with Rhodesia.[73] They wondered whether the new measure could appropriately be justified on the basis of actual need for chrome since, at the time of the legislation, the US had an excess rather than a shortage of chrome ore available for defense needs. As evidence they cited the administration's request to release for civilian consumption more than 1.3 million tons of chrome ore held in military stockpiles.[74] In August, 1970, the Office of Emergency Preparedness had concluded that "the domestic ferroalloy capacity continues to be sufficient to meet emergency defense and civilian requirements."[75]

The purchase of Rhodesian chrome brought Nixon under fire from African governments as well as American liberals and blacks, who felt that the US action undermined the sanctions imposed by the UN. Even Secretary of State William Rogers admitted, on March 26, 1972, that

> Sanctions have placed some strains on the Rhodesian economy. They have brought a 30 percent loss in the total value of foreign trade, reduced foreign-exchange earnings by almost two-thirds and caused the regime to impose controls on economic growth.[76]

Although the legislation was initiated by Senator Harry F. Byrd (Ind—Virginia) in Congress, the Nixon administration apparently concurred with this pro-Rhodesia change in US policy. Neither Nixon nor Kissinger made public statements to defend US compliance with the UN sanctions. During this period, the White House was being pressured by Congressional Republican leadership, including Strom Thurmond (R—South Carolina) and Harry Byrd (Ind—Virginia) to authorize the purchase of chrome from the white minority regime in Salisbury. The ferrochromium industry was also pressuring the White House to lift the US ban on Rhodesian chrome. As a result, Nixon did not veto the bill, a privilege he had often exercised when in disagreement with Congress, nor had his administration attempted to pull any strings to defeat the Byrd amendment.[77]

It should be remembered that the Department of State had argued against the proposed legislation, on the basis that it violated international law and also that "the embargo has not created serious economic problems for the United States."[78] When the White House did not accept this argument, opposition to the Byrd amendment was left in the hands of middle- and low-level officials in the State Department, who generally understood that "we wouldn't be getting any medals from the White House [for this task]'"[79] Opposition within the Nixon administration subsided after the appointment of former Union Carbide president Kenneth Rush as Deputy Secretary of State.

The Department of State played a minor role in the shaping of US-Rhodesian policy. It is likely that Nixon's views on the Byrd amendment were developed primarily in consultation with White House staff and advisors. It is also rumored that Dean Acheson had a major influence on White House views on southern Africa and, until his death in October, 1971, on White House decisions with regard to the region. Indeed, it has been widely assumed that Option 1, the most extreme policy option in terms of its pro-white orientation, was generally known as the "Dean Acheson option."[80] Acheson was an outspoken partisan in favor of white minority rule in southern Africa, and the Byrd Amendment represented a strong move in support of the white minority regime in Rhodesia at a time when the majority of the nations were abiding by the UN call for an embargo on such materials as chrome ore.[81]

British Prime Minister Harold Wilson commented in 1972 on the Nixon decision to allow the importation of Rhodesian chrome that he "[could] think of no act more calculated to outrage moderate African feeling and to give aid and comfort to racialists south of the Zambezi and indeed north and south of the Limpopo."[82] The US, however, might have been motivated by the desire to back Britain's settlement plans, under negotiation at the time, with a source of economic incentive for Rhodesia. Thus, it seems that Nixon largely continued to follow and be supportive of Britain's stance on Rhodesia, much as the Johnson administration had done. Despite opposition from African leaders on the settlement terms which Britain was developing with Rhodesia, the US generally supported these terms. Thus, on February 4, 1972, the US abstained on an African resolution in the Security Council urging Britain to scrap its settlement plans and to convene a constitutional conference to decide Rhodesia's future.[83]

The Nixon administration was largely indifferent to repeal efforts despite the fact that Kissinger, at his confirmation hearings as Secretary of State, promised that "The administration will support the repeal of the Byrd Amendment."[84] This promise was not translated into action, however. Senator Gale McGee (D—Wyoming) criticized Nixon's failure to give active support to his efforts to repeal the Byrd Amendment after he had been assured of White House support. He blamed the White House's neutrality for the defeat in 1972 of his bill to repeal the law. Senator McGee furiously remarked:

> I personally appealed to the White House for assistance. I asked that they make only five or six telephone calls to marginal Senators on the Administration's side of the Senate aisle — several of whom had already told me a 'call from the administration would be necessary to change my vote.' As it turned out, the White House would have had to make only three calls to turn the tide in our favor. . . . But no call was forthcoming. The Administration had put its rhetoric behind the McGee bill and the UN, but did not lift the telephone even once to back that rhetoric up.[85]

The same sentiment was expressed in the *New York Times*, which stated:

> The Senate behavior reflected a double game by the Nixon administration. It tried to placate liberals, blacks, UN backers and African governments with a State Department letter supporting Mr. McGee while refusing them the minimal White House initiative that would have brought him victory.[86]

Despite the mounting domestic opposition, the Nixon administration decided to resume the importation of Rhodesian chrome. As outlined in Annex 4 of the NSSM document, this measure was assumed to ease the hard pressed US ferroalloy industries and would benefit two American companies — Foote Mineral and Union Carbide — which had been unable to operate their mines in Rhodesia because of the Johnson administration's adherence to UN Rhodesian sanctions. It was expected that the importation of Rhodesian chrome would make the US less dependent on the Soviet Union, which had supplied the US with about 50 percent of imported chrome, and might force down the price of chrome, which had doubled between 1967 and 1972[87] It is interesting to note that much of the argument in favor of the importation of Rhodesian chrome centered among "protectionist interests who saw the issue solely in dollars-and-cents terms."[88]

It has been reported that, since 1972, US imports from Rhodesia have amounted to roughly 10 percent of total US chromite imports and, second, that imports from Soviet chrome have remained at the same level. Third, there has been a decline in chromite purchases from other countries.[89] The Byrd Amendment thus failed to break the US dependency on the Soviet Union for this strategic and critical material.

As for Rhodesia, the Nixon administration must have been aware of the economic implications of its decision to allow the importation of Rhodesian chrome. Annex 3 of NSSM 39 briefly but accurately analyzed the effect of UN sanctions on the Rhodesian economy and described the dim economic picture of Rhodesia in 1969, which had caused many Rhodesian businessmen to urge Smith "to negotiate a settlement to end sanctions."[90] The US decision to lift the ban was poorly timed since it might have eased Rhodesia's economic crunch and encouraged Smith to hold out indefinitely by weakening the opposition, which had stood for a settlement to end sanctions. Nixon's decision to violate the UN sanctions was a major psychological boost, not only to the Smith regime but also to all white minority regimes in southern Africa, since it linked the US with South Africa and Portugal, both of whom NSSM 39 had identified as persistent violators of UN sanctions.[91]

Nixon's implementation of the sanctions program had been "lethargic, ineffective and passive at best."[92] Massive violations of sanctions were reported in areas such as airline bookings, car rentals, credit cards, investment advertisements and tourism. For all practical purposes, these violations were not prosecuted and no attempt was made to bring them to a halt. A recent study revealed that American visitors to Rhodesia constituted one-fifth of that country's tourist trade with a net value of a little over $16 million annually in foreign exchange.[93] Neither the Department of Justice nor Treasury attempted to close down the Rhodesian Information Office; instead, it was allowed to disseminate information, to lobby on Capitol Hill, to encourage American tourism and to recruit Americans to work for Rhodesia's armed forces. Moreover, the Air Rhodesia office in New York continued to work closely with American airlines, travel agencies and credit-card companies.[94] The Nixon administration closed its eyes to all of these violations which, together, gave the Smith regime a material and psychological lift at a time when the Rhodesian economy was weak and when domestic opposition had been mounting in favor of a compromise settlement.

ANGOLA AND MOZAMBIQUE

The Portuguese tilt of the Nixon-Kissinger policy stemmed from the strategic military importance of the Azores and the Portuguese African colonies to American cold-war defense planning.[95] US military interests in maintaining Portugal's friendship as a NATO ally thus served as the guiding factor influencing American policy toward Angola and Mozambique. David M. Abshire, in his discussion of the strategic role of the Portuguese possessions, has put forward some relevant insights. As he pointed out:

> Because of their pivotal positions, the Portuguese possessions could become economically and strategically important in certain conflict situations. Military patrol aircraft operating from these areas could effectively survey the eastern South Atlantic, the Western Indian Ocean and the seas south of the Cape.

And in referring to their economic importance, he noted:

> Angola serves as the door to one of the most minerally rich parts of Africa. Mozambique has become a door of equal or greater importance for draining the Copper belt and other productive areas of Zambia, Rhodesia, and Transvaal. Both Angola and Mozambique secure the strategic flanks of South Africa, the wealthiest and most powerful area in Africa and the most sensitive in terms of US and UK policies.[96]

In the late 1960s, Luso-American relations took a turn for the better with two events: the inauguration of President Nixon and the end of the Salazar regime. The new Prime Minister, Marcello Caetano, moved to mend fences with Washington, but Nixon first had to work out his stance toward the two conflicting purposes – US economic and strategic interests versus African self-determination – that had also faced his predecessors in office. The pro-African policy initiated by the Kennedy administration had to be reevaluated, particularly in the context of conservative and pro-business Republican interests.[97]

NSSM 39 was helpful in swinging the views of the Republican administration in favor of a policy that would "reduce a major irritant in our relations with Portugal and afford the Caetano government opportunity for liberalization."[98] As outlined in Option 2, this policy could be designed to "continue [the] arms embargo on Portuguese territories, but give more liberal treatment to exports of dual purpose equipment" and to "encourage trade and investment in Portuguese territories; full EXIM Bank facilities."[99]

The Nixon administration's decision was to give Caetano some time to get his house in order. The administration was to pursue a "quiet policy of more relaxed relations" and keep a low profile on its opposition to Portugal's African stance. The hope was that, by increased communication and "selective involvement" the US might encourage the new regime in Lisbon to bring about change in southern Africa.[100]

The new policy had its impact on American voting behavior in the United Nations. In the next months, the US voted against several African-sponsored resolutions proposing that Portugal be condemned for not recognizing the right of the people in the Portuguese territories to self-determination and independence, expressing concern over the intensification of foreign economic activites there and appealing for a stop in the training of Portuguese military personnel and the sale of arms.[101] A comment in the *Economist* noted that "Nixon's administration . . . used the veto more freely than its predecessors."[102]

Starting in 1970, the Nixon administration also moved to "stifle any criticism of Portugal's colonial role in Africa by more liberal members of NATO such as Norway and Canada, a strategy which [would] in fact enable a more silent and cohesive coordination of aid to Portugal."[103] This was an aspect of the concerted efforts by the US to extend the NATO zone as far south as the Cape of Good Hope to combat the growing presence of Soviet naval power in the Indian Ocean. At about the same time, Portugal's Defense Minister Rebelo offered NATO the use of its "territories and bases outside the NATO zone," which "could help control the vast area of the whole Atlantic."[104]

The Nixon doctrine calling for "regional and defense arrangements which provide and take advantage of shared responsibilities" was welcomed by Prime Minister Caetano. He interpreted Nixon's call for defense to be "assumed by local and regional forces" to mean that NATO should openly support Portugal in its colonial wars in Angola, Guinea

(Bissau) and Mozambique. Caetano, in his *Guidelines of Foreign Policy* 1970), stated that

> The West is a bloc, but this solidarity cannot be limited to a few matters located on the territory of Europe. . . . At all times and everywhere in the world its values or vital interests are threatened, we have the duty of defending them.[105]

As John Marcum has noted, the Azores fit very well into the Nixon doctrine emphasis on "strategic retrenchment into detached or insular bases" in a way that a "potent military outreach" could still be maintained.[106]

In December, 1971, in line with NSSM 39, President Nixon signed an executive agreement with Portugal. In exchange for utilization of the Azores base, the agreement authorized the US Export-Import Bank to extend a credit-loan to Portugal of $436 million, a figure four times the total amount the Export-Import Bank had extended to Portugal between 1946 and 1971. It was a five-year accord and was made retroactive to 1969, the date when initial written communication was exchanged between the two governments.[107]

The terms of the agreement represented a substantial change in American foreign policy in a direction strongly favorable to Portugal. Such a move was very much in line with Kissinger's interest in NATO, with his overriding concern with the Troubled Partnership and with his vast and deliberate efforts to revise the North Atlantic Charter. Aside from the strategic value of the Azores, Portugal's NATO membership was undoubtedly an important factor in the Nixon Administration's decision and must be viewed in the context of Kissinger's grand design for strengthening NATO members economically and militarily prior to the conclusion of SALT talks and the subsequent reduction of American troop strength in Europe.[108]

NSSM 39 also had its impact on Nixon's arms embargo against the Portuguese territories. In 1970, revised guidelines were issued permitting "more liberal treatment" of dual purpose equipment (i.e. that could be used for civilian or military purposes), a position suggested by Option 2 of NSSM 39. Subsequently, Portugal was able to purchase helicopters, aircraft, large airliners and other equipment that could be converted to military usage as the need arose[109] (Table 4). Between 1971 and 1972, for example, the Nixon administration authorized the direct sale of two Boeing 707s and two Boeing 747s to Portugal for use as military transport planes in Africa. Moreover, the Export-Import Bank approved loans and guarantees supporting the sale of twelve Bell helicopters to Lisbon (for use in Mozambique) as well as the sale of a number of Rockwell photo-reconnaisance aircraft through the coopera-

tive financing arrangement extended to Portugal under the Azores
Agreement.[110]

Table 4

Exports of American Aircraft and Helicopters
to Angola, Mozambique, and Portugal: 1965-1972

Year	Angola		Mozambique		Portugal	
	No.	*Value*	*No.*	*Value*	*No.*	*Value*
		$		$		$
1965	5	209,940	1	23,177	5	7,021,428
1966	7	248,196	—	—	1	14,667
1967	16	360,647	—	—	7	14,132,912
1968	11	303,556	1	105,122	14	25,370,505
1969	5	211,056	2	7,576,956	9	7,753,035
1970	12	477,797	21	808,030	10	16,458,548
1971	23	513,908	1	5,143,175	9	10,487,256
1972	—	—	13	881,678	10	57,936,468
Subtotal 1965-68:	39	1,122,339	2	128,299	27	46,539,512
Subtotal 1969-72	40	1,202,761	37	14,409,839	38	92,635,307

Source: Bureau of the Census, FT-410 Export Statistics

The Nixon administration provided Portugal with military assistance, averaging about one million dollars per annum, and continued
its training of Portuguese military personnel. Table 5 reveals that the
number of Portuguese trained by Americans at home and abroad almost
doubled during the first year of the Nixon administraton, from 74 in
1968 to 130 in 1969. Further, while American training largely concentrated on naval personnel between 1968 and 1970, by 1971 the

United States had begun to provide a substantial amount of training for Portugal's air force officers. In addition, the US began to increase substantially its delivery of defoliation chemicals (i.e. herbicides), which were used by Portuguese forces in Africa. As documented in Table 6, the export of herbicides to Portugal was six times greater in 1970 than in 1969; herbicide exports to Mozambique in 1972 were about five times higher than the level of the year before.

Table 5

Number of Portuguese Military Personnel Trained
by the US: Fiscal Year 1968-1972 Inclusive

Year	Army US	Overseas	Air Force US	Overseas	Navy US	Overseas	Total
1968	6	4	1	—	63	—	74
1969	3	25	7	—	95	—	130
1970	8	29	2	—	49	—	88
1971	6	31	3	45	18	—	103
1972	6	30	10	17	16	—	79
1973	15	35	12	17	15	—	94
Total	44	154	35	79	256	—	568

Source: Implementation of the US Arms Embargo (Against Portugal and South Africa, and Related Issues). Hearings before the Subcommittee on Africa of the Committee on Foreign Affairs, House of Representatives, 93d Congress, 1st session, March 20, 22; April 6, 1973. (Washington, DC: US Government Printing Office, 1973.) p. 89.

The Nixon years also witnessed the consistent growth of American private investment in Angola and Mozambique. The outstanding example is Cabinda Gulf Oil, the largest single foreign investor in Portuguese Africa. Largely because of the Gulf Oil investment, the US was already Angola's second major supplier in 1968 (with 11.8 percent of imports), outranked by Portugal but followed closely by West Germany (11.1

percent) and Britain (8.9 percent). In the following years, the American share of Angola's market rose steadily: imports from the US increased by 17.2 percent in 1970 and a further 16.5 percent in 1971, primarily due to increased importation of capital goods, raw materials and partly finished goods for local industries.[111]

Table 6

US Exports of Herbicides to Angola,
Mozambique and Portugal, 1962-72
(In millions of dollars)

Year	Angola	Mozambique	Portugal
1969	2	—	57
1970	43	28	344
1971	—	88	115
1972	39	413	151
Total	84	529	667

Source: "Portugal Afrique: La Guerre de L'OTAN" *Jeune Afrique* No. 705, July 13, 1974, p. 64.

Gulf estimated its total investments in 1972 to be worth $209 million and reported that its exports of crude oil had jumped from 4.7 million tons in 1971 to 6.8 million in 1972 (an increase of 43.9 percent), bringing in approximately $167 million in foreign currency, the equivalent of 25.4 percent of all Angola's export earnings. It was reported that, in 1972 alone, Gulf paid the Portuguese authorities in Angola $61 million in income taxes and royalties; in comparison, for the entire period between 1968 and 1972, payments by Gulf had totalled $96.7 million. Gulf Oil signed an additional contract in 1972, allowing it to expand its activities into prospecting for and exploitation of sulphur, helium and carbon dioxide in Angola.[112]

In the early seventies, a growing number of American companies sought access to petroleum concessions in Angola. These included the

Ranger Oil Company of Cheyenne, Superior Oil Company of Houston, Carlsberg Resources Corporation (Los Angeles), the Milford Argosy Corporation of North Portland, Esso Exploration, Incorporated of Houston, and Iberian Petroleum Limited of Stanford. In addition, Western Geophysical Company, a subsidiary of Litton Industries, was subcontracted by Angola to carry out part of its prospecting activities offshore in the Congo area. Further, Texaco continued its prospecting operations with ANGOL, PETRANGOL and TOTAL. It was also reported that ANGOL-PETRANGOL had negotiated with a group of foreign companies to increase offshore prospecting activities in the Cuanza area.[113]

Angola's potential mineral wealth was the primary object of investor interest. Portugal's encouragement of foreign capital resulted in much competitive activity by American and European multinational corporations for the exploration and development of possible deposits of iron ore, diamonds, sulphur and phosphates. In 1969, three American firms – Diversa, Incorporated, Diamond Distributors of New York and DIAMUL – were granted concessions for diamond prospecting and exploration in southwestern Angola. The Rockefeller group, represented by the Clark Canadian Exploration Company, holds one-third of the share capital of the Companhia dos Fosfatos de Angola (COFAN), which began phosphate prospecting in Cabinda in 1969. In May, 1972, the Great Lakes Carbon Corporation of New York applied for a concession to prospect for and exploit copper deposits in Cuanza (North Districts). That same year, Argo Petroleum Corporation of Los Angeles received a concession covering five areas totalling 12,189 square kilometers. In 1973, the Riverwood Corporation of Midland Texas was contracted by the Companhia dos Asfaltos de Angola for the exploitation of rock asphalt.[114]

In regard to Mozambique, Bethlehem Steel and its consortium partners obtained an exclusive concession in 1972 for mineral prospecting between Djanguire to Changara in the Tete District. In the same year, the Export-Import Bank granted an investment loan of a little over a million dollars to the Banco Commercial e Industrial de Laurenco Marques. Hunt International Petroleum Company and Mozambique Amoco Oil Company are currently involved in oil prospecting and exploitation.[115]

This stepped-up pace of American economic activity in Portuguese Africa came under considerable criticism. Most notably, the United Presbyterian Church and other church groups started a drive in 1971 to solicit proxy votes from Gulf Oil Corporation stockholders in order to force Gulf to suspend its Cabinda operations. A year later, the World Council of Churches voted to sell its stock in companies that did business with white minority regimes in southern Africa.[116]

Criticism for Nixon's southern African policy was also voiced by African leaders. They opposed US investment in and trade with Portuguese Africa as well as its military assistance to Portugal on the ground that this aid released other Portuguese resources for use in suppressing African rights and freedom. They argued, moreover, that NATO equipment had been illegally used by Portugal to repress African liberation movements in southern Africa.

Nevertheless, the Nixon strategy of trying to improve the atmosphere of Portuguese-American relations was partially rewarded during the Yom Kippur war in the Middle East. When the US decided to airlift arms to Israel in October, 1973, Portugal was the only NATO ally which allowed American planes bound for Israel to refuel on its territory. Caetano's decision to assist the US, and to allow use of the Azores base, rested on his desire to demonstrate to the Americans that Portugal was a reliable ally; he hoped that the US could in turn give his country diplomatic and moral support in its efforts to retain its African colonies.[117]

In April, 1974, the overthrow of Caetano's regime by the Portuguese military created a fluid and potentially dangerous situation for US interests. Although the provisional President — General Antonio de Spinola — could be termed a moderate conservative, the Nixon administration decided to withhold open support for the new Portuguese government, apparently out of fear that the country might fall under communist influence.

Portuguese interests in maintaining American friendship did not immediately change under the Armed Forces Movement. Although some observers had commented that Portugal would no longer need American diplomatic and military support when the decolonization process was completed in Africa, it was all the more evident that the loss of the African territories would mean that Porgugal would likely become more dependent on economic aid from the US and Western Europe.

Toward the end of the Nixon era, Portuguese-American relations grew stronger as his administration presented a stance of understanding and appreciation for Portugal's colonial problems in Africa. The US continued to call publicly for a rejection of violence as a means for national liberation and insisted on the need to reach a negotiated settlement. As Nixon stated: "While we favor change, we do not regard violence as an acceptable formula for common progress."[118]

FORD'S POLICY TOWARD SOUTHERN AFRICA

Nixon's abrupt departure from the White House did not result in any immediate changes in US policy toward southern Africa, largely because Kissinger continued to dominate policy decision-making in the new Ford administration. In the first few months of his term, Ford paid little or no attention to southern African problems because he was pre-occupied with the economy and public confidence in the Presidency in the aftermath of the Watergate scandal. In turn, Secretary of State Kissinger was totally absorbed in his efforts to conclude a second inter-im agreement between Egypt and Israel. Under these circumstances, foreign policy regarding southern Africa was left in the hands of other State Department officials who, while mindful that the basis for NSSM 39's analysis had been eroded by changes in southern Africa since the Portuguese coup of April, 1974, were not free to make major changes on their own.

SOUTH AFRICA

President Ford continued the Nixon policy of communication with white minority regimes in southern Africa. William Bowdler, his appointee as US Ambassador to South Africa, told the Senate Foreign Relations Committee in March, 1975, that he anticipated no major changes in US policy toward Pretoria because "our policy of communi-cation and dialogue is of great importance to us."[119] Like Nixon, Presi-dent Ford also continued to permit visits by top South African officials to Washington. In June, 1975, South Africa's Minister of Information Mulder met with Assistant Secretary Nathaniel Davis and with several Congressmen sympathetic towards South Africa. Enroute home, Mulder made an unexplained stopover in Honolulu at the headquarters of CINCPAC, the US Navy's Pacific Command which is responsible for Indian Ocean security.[120]

US officials — particularly conservative Congressmen — also were permitted to take South-African sponsored trips to meet with top lead-ers there. For example, in March, 1975, a delegation that included two members of the House Armed Services Committee met with Mulder and various South African military commanders.[121] A by-product of these visits has been a growing effort by various Congressmen to strength-en US-South African relations, especially in terms of the arms embargo.

In May, 1975, Secretary of Defense James Schlesinger proposed at a conference of NATO defense ministers that NATO should make arrangements to use the Simonstown base and establish a monitoring installation in South Africa for intelligence purposes.[122] The growing interest of the US in Diego Garcia had already drawn South Africa deeply into American strategic planning.

The close relationship between Washington and Pretoria had its impact on US voting behavior in the United Nations. On October 30, 1974, the US joined Britain and France in an unprecedented triple veto when they jointly rejected a Security Council resolution calling for the expulsion of South Africa from the world body. This was followed a month later by another negative vote by the US in the Special Committee on a resolution requesting the Security Council to meet on the race question in South Africa and to take mandatory action to halt all arms supplies to Pretoria.[123] This United States was the only member casting a negative vote on the resolution.

This voting trend has continued throughout the Ford years. On June 6, 1975, the US once again joined Britain and France in another triple veto on a Security Council resolution that would have imposed a mandatory arms embargo on South Africa in order to help bring about the independence of Namibia. In defending this position, Ambassador Jonn A. Scali stated: "We believe that mandatory sanctions . . . should be reserved for the most acute and critical threats to . . . peace. Although we fundamentally disagree with certain actions by South Africa, we do not consider that the situation has reached such a critical state."[124]

For South Africa, faced with growing diplomatic isolation, the US position provided a valuable boost for national morale. David Ottaway reported from Johannesburg on June 4, 1975, that "not many countries are lending support to the Pretoria government these days, and the positions taken by the United States, France and Britain . . . are viewed as crucial for averting further international action against South Africa and for allowing it to settle the Namibia issue on its own terms."[125]

RHODESIA (ZIMBABWE)

The Ford administration has so far failed to translate its repeated promises into active support of Congressional efforts to repeal the Byrd Amendment. In August, 1974, President Ford made a strong statement in favor of the repeal[126] and promised the Black Congressional Caucus that he would lobby among Republicans toward that end. He changed his mind, however, and backed away from a pledge to send personal letters to key Republican members of the House of Representatives urging them to support the repeal bill. Without the President's support, the sponsors of the bill decided to withdraw it "minutes before it was scheduled for consideration" because there were not sufficient votes for its passage.[127]

During 1975, Kissinger continued to suggest that the Ford administration was in favor of repeal efforts. On September 23, 1975, for example, he told the OAU representatives in New York that "President Ford and his entire cabinet continue to urge repeal of the Byrd Amendment and expect this will be accomplished during the current session of the Congress."[128] Only two days dater, the measure was defeated in the House by a margin of 22 votes.

Critics accused the administration of practicing deception because "up until the morning of the vote, the White House told the bill's sponsors that they would lobby on their behalf, but they did not contact one 'swing' member of Congress to urge him or her to vote for H.R. 1287."[129] Table 7 shows that only 22 out of the 145 Republicans voted for the bill. Of the 108 negative votes cast by Republicans, some might have been swayed to change their votes if they had received telephone calls or personal letters from the White House. The Washington Office on Africa, which has actively lobbied for the repeal since 1972, accused the administration of partial responsibility for the defeat because it had failed "to act on its statements of support for sanctions. Throughout the three-year sanctions battle, the White House dangled the carrot of its support before the bill's sponsors, who always knew that the margin of victory or defeat would be small."[130]

Table 7

Pattern of Voting to Repeal the Byrd Amendment (H.R. 1287)
in the House of Representatives: 94th Congress

	Yes		No		Abstention		Total	
	No.	%	No.	%	No.	%	No.	%
Democrats	165	57.3	101	35.1	22	7.6	288	100
Republicans	22	15.2	108	74.5	15	10.3	145	100
Total	187	43.2	209	48.3	37	8.5	433	100

Many Senators and Congressmen have urged Ford to work more actively toward repeal of the Byrd Amendment. Representative Donald Fraser (D — Minnesota) has advised the administration to start thinking of the prospects for long-term access to Rhodesian chrome. Without a basic change in the present policy, he argued, the US might not be able to purchase chrome from a majority government in the future. Moreover, he stressed that the US might jeopardize its relations throughout Africa — affecting accessibility to such other critical African minerals as Nigeria's oil — because of its defiance of UN sanctions against Rhodesia.[131] Representative John B. Anderson (R — Illinois) has suggested that repeal of the Byrd Amendment at this time "can assist in getting negotiations back on the track and thus enhance the prospects of a peaceful settlement." He concluded that failure to do so would "exacerbate the problem and invite violence by bolstering the barriers to majority rule."[132]

There are signs that the Ford administration is beginning to support US compliance with the UN sanctions. Early in 1976, the US co-sponsored a Security Council resolution expanding mandatory sanctions against Rhodesia. Then in March, the US commended Mozambique for its decision to enforce UN sanctions by closing its 800-mile border with Rhodesia. The Ford administration later expressed its willingness to provide Mozambique with some aid to ease the revenue loss occurring from closing down its transit facilities for Rhodesian shipment.[133]

MOZAMBIQUE AND ANGOLA

With Mozambique on the way to independence, the US began mending fences with FRELIMO leaders. Assistant Secretary for African Affairs Donald Easum was strongly interested in moving the US away from NSSM 39 policy and in making changes that would be more responsive to the needs of black Africans. His direct efforts were the basis for whatever short-term success the US has recently had in improving its relations with Mozambique. His conciliatory approach and insistence on a progressive US policy — based on support for majority rule in southern Africa — was able to convince Mozambique's new leaders that the US wished to improve its image after long years of siding with Portugal. In November, 1974, Easum met with Samora Machel in Tanzania and with Joaquim Chissano, Prime Minister of the transitional government, inside Mozambique. He was thus the first foreign diplomat to meet with the newly formed government.[134]

Easum was relieved of his position shortly after his return from southern Africa, however, and Nathaniel Davis, a former US Ambassador to Chile — and an accused participant in the "destabilization programs" against the legitimate government of Salvador Allende — was appointed in his place. This change was interpreted by some observers as a move by Kissinger to dissociate himself from Easum's advocacy of a policy supporting majority rule in southern Africa. Such a new stance would represent a strong departure from the long-term Nixon and Kissinger policy (embodied in the NSSM document) that stressed "regional stability" at the cost of majority rule.[135]

One immediate result was a cooling off in the US-Mozambican relationship. The US was not invited, for instance, to participate in the celebration of Mozambican independence.* Further, despite the fact that Washington has extended recognition to the FRELIMO government, Mozambique has not yet sent its ambassador to Washington.

The Angolan War

In Mozambique, the Ford administration had been forced to accept the leadership of the Marxist-leaning movement, because there was no other viable alternative after the collapse of the rival COREMO (which had been encouraged by the American embassy in Zambia to organize an anti-FRELIMO coalition inside Mozambique).[136] In Angola, the situation was entirely different, with three liberation movements — the FNLA, the MPLA and the UNITA — competing for power. Initially, the Ford administration was interested in blocking the ascendance of the Soviet-backed movement, the MPLA, in minerally rich and strategically located Angola. It consequently monitored closely the fate of the transitional government, which attempted to have the three liberation movements work together. The existence of major ethnic, tribal and ideological cleavages among Angola's leaders made such a coalition unworkable, however, and also provided an inviting arena for outside influence. The US, South Africa, Zaire, Zambia and China sided with the FNLA-UNITA factions, while the Soviet Union, Cuba and Mozambique took the other side. Each major world power entered the conflict largely out of fear that the other might take advantage of the detente and attempt to increase its sphere of influence in southern Africa.

From the outset, foreign intervention took place along ideological lines. Massive Soviet and Cuban support of the MPLA, which began in the fall of 1975, provoked a strong public reaction from the Ford administration. In a speech in Detroit on November 24, 1975, Secretary of State Kissinger expressed displeasure over "the substantial Soviet buildup in Angola which has introduced great-power rivalry into Africa for the first time in 15 years."[137] A month later, President Ford warned Moscow that "its aid and the dispatch of several thousand Cuban military advisors to support its faction in Angola could jeopardize detente." [138]

Contrary to public statements implying American intervention in Angola was a response to Soviet initiatives, covert US operations in Angola had begun as early as January, 1975. The White House, on the basis

---

* Representative Charles C. Diggs, Jr., former chairman of the House Subcommittee on Africa, was invited and attended the celebration as a private citizen in recognition of his long support for the liberation struggle in Africa.

of a recommendation by the National Security Council's Forty Committee on covert intelligence, decided to provide $300,000 and military equipment to the FNLA through the CIA. This initial amount, "thirty times larger than any US annual sum ever given Roberto"[139] before, represented a significant escalation of American involvement. By the fall, aid had risen to $35 million to provide arms and supplies to the anticommunist factions in Angola (see Appendix A). Non-American weapons from CIA supplies were delivered to the Western-backed factions to conceal their American origins.[140] The July decision to expand the CIA's covert operations inside Angola,* which had been the first of several decisions that brought US aid into the level of millions of dollars, had coincided with UNITA's withdrawal from the coalition government and with South Africa's military intervention there.[141]

The primary objective for the US was to sustain the FNLA role in the transitional government in order to counterbalance the growing influence of the socialist-leaning MPLA. The Ford administration was afraid that, if the MPLA succeeded in coming to power alone, the Soviet Union would gain an important foothold in southern Africa and consequently might get air and sea bases on Angola's West African coast. That, in conjunction with the Russian airfields in Guinea, would ensure Soviet domination of the South Atlantic including command of the oil shipping lanes around the Cape of Good Hope.[142] Furthermore, a Soviet-backed regime in Angola could manipulate the country's oil and mineral resources.

For all these reasons, the Ford administration funneled a total of fifty to sixty million dollars worth of arms and support funds to the anti-MPLA faction in Angola.[143] Most of the American aid was channeled through Zaire. Both governments wanted to "stop Russian domination" in Angola by limiting the MPLA's influence and by installing an FNLA and/or UNITA regime in Luanda. President Mobutu Sese Seko worked closely with the CIA in directing American military and financial assistance to the anti-MPLA forces, particularly to the groups in the northern region that were led by his brother-in-law, Holden Roberto, long known for his CIA connections.

By late November, 1975, the US began to intensify its public campaign against Soviet and Cuban intervention. It requested additional funds from Congress for covert CIA operations in Angola to help reverse the military setbacks caused by the massive Soviet buildup of

---

* This escalation of US military involvement in Angola, it should be noted, was against the judgment of Nathaniel Davis, then Assistant Secretary of State for African Affairs, who stressed the need for a "diplomatic approach" to the Angolan crisis. See Seymour M. Hersh, "Angola-Aid Issue Opening Rifts in State Department," *The New York Times*, December 14, 1975.

weapons and Cuban armed intervention in support of the MPLA. The US also pressured countries like Trinidad and Tobago and Barbados to deny refueling privileges to Cuban planes enroute to Luanda. Moreover, the Gulf Oil Company was asked to suspend operations in Cabinda rather than give the MPLA the quarterly royalty and tax payments of $100 million due in December, 1975.

The Ford administration ran into strong opposition from the US Senate, however. In December, 1975, the Senate refused to appropriate more funds to aid the pro-Western factions in Angola. The administration was therefore put on notice that it faced an uphill battle to get the US House of Representatives to overturn the Senate ban on military assistance.

The White House was encouraged in this effort by the fact that the OAU Summit Conference (January, 1976) failed to find a solution to the Angolan crisis, and that twenty-two African nations had agreed with the US stance that a three-way government of national unity should be formed. Facilitating the administration's task even further was Pretoria's announcement that it would pull out of Angola if other foreign troops would do likewise.[144] This timely announcement was made during deliberations by the House of Representatives on whether or not to uphold the Senate ban on covert aid to the FNLA-UNITA factions. Armed with Pretoria's statement, Kissinger argued that continuing American involvement in Angola was needed in order to halt Soviet expansion in southern Africa and to give token support to South Africa, which was becoming increasingly reluctant to be trapped alone in an endless war in Angola. He concluded that US aid could serve as an ultimatum to the Soviet Union and Cuba and could give the Ford administration some leverage by which to negotiate a diplomatic solution to the Angolan crisis.

Neither Pretoria's decaration about withdrawal from Angola nor Kissinger's argument was sufficient to rally the votes needed to overturn the Senate ban. On January 27, 1976, despite a last-minute appeal by President Ford, the House voted 323 to 99 to ban covert military aid to Angola. The Ford administration was ordered not to spend any funds on military support to groups fighting in Angola.[145] The frustrated President accused the Congress of having "lost its guts."[146]

The fact of Washington and Pretoria on the same side in the Angolan conflict created a controversy in the United States. Daniel P. Moynihan, US Ambassador to the UN, defended the joint effort stating, "There is a convergence in policy. We are both doing the same thing, sort of."[147] But others felt that the US should have pursued a "hands-off" policy, ceasing aid of any kind.[148] They were critical of both the covert US aid and South African military intervention which, in their views, were not coincidental. They cited several sources of indirect evidence, including close cooperation between the CIA and the South African security service on a long-term basis[149] and a statement made by a South African official, quoted in the *New York Times*, that the invasion was launched after contacts with US officials had indicated that support would be forthcoming.[150]

TOWARD A NEW US-SOUTHERN AFRICAN POLICY

By the end of 1974, it was becoming unrealistic for the Ford administration to base its policy on the guidelines of NSSM 39. The Portuguese coup of April, 1974, had set in motion the independence of its African territories and, consequently, had dramatically changed the balance of power between blacks and whites in southern Africa. Mozambican independence meant that, except for South Africa, land-locked Rhodesia was surrounded by black-ruled nations and could expect to come under increasing military and economic pressures by them. Similarly, the victory of the MPLA in Angola signalled trouble for South Africa in Namibia because the SWAPO could rely on military and financial assistance from the new government in Luanda and could freely use southern Angola as a sanctuary for an escalated military campaign against South Africa's illegal administration of Namibia. The changes in Mozambique and Angola have an impact on South Africa because, with black-ruled nations along the borders of both South Africa and Namibia, the white minority regimes were more vulnerable to guerrilla attacks.

The presence of 12,000 to 15,000 Cubans in Angola — ready to be used against white minority regimes in the area — created a further dilemma for the United States. On the one hand, the Ford administration had limited leverage in southern Africa. It had no substantial presence there and the Congressional ban on aid to Angola has led some observers to think that the US would not be able to prevent outside intervention in future African conflicts.[151] On the other hand, the Ford administration could not just sit back and allow Cuban troops to be used in a black-white confrontation in that region. Cuban intervention could occur in either Namibia or Rhodesia, a situation that might eventually lead to the Soviet-American confrontation that Kissinger has worked so hard to avoid. Under these circumstances, the Ford administration must take some new initiatives, first, to dispel any doubt about its ability to discourage Cuba from further military adventures in southern Africa and, secondly, to halt pressures by white minority regimes to give them at least indirect aid to curtail Cuban-Soviet expansion (see Appendix A).

These new developments have invalidated the basic premise of

Option 2 of NSSM 39 that white regimes could not be toppled. Following the Angolan debacle, President Ford ordered Kissinger to review US-southern African relations and to prepare a new policy taking into account the recent events in the area, particularly the presence of massive Cuban forces in Angola and the substantial increase in Soviet influence and prestige. While the new policy was being formulated, the Ford administration repeatedly warned the Soviet Union and Cuba against military adventures in Africa, making it clear that US-Soviet detente could not survive "another Angola."[152] As Kissinger stated in March, 1976, "The United States will not accept further Communist military intervention in Africa."[153] He also declared that the Ford administration would take decisive action against further Cuban intervention in Africa or elsewhere. Moreover, he ordered the NSC to review options open to the US in the political, economic and military areas and requested that the Joint Chiefs of Staff review several contingencies regarding Cuban troops.[154]

These measures drew criticism from Congressional leaders. Senate Majority Leader Mike Mansfield described Kissinger's remarks as "useless rhetoric" and "rhetoric which may be dangerous."[155] House Majority Leader Thomas P. O'Neil, Jr. demanded that Ford "publicly repudiate or explain statements by Secretary of State Henry A. Kissinger and the White House."[156] This strong Congressional reaction forced the administration to soften its stance. Secretary of Defense Donald H. Rumsfeld shortly stated that they were reviewing "only economic or political action against Cuba, not military."[157]

The challenge to the Ford administration is to get Cuban troops out of Angola while also finding ways to help bring about a speedy and peaceful transfer of power in Rhodesia and Namibia. The new policy must deal with both of these problems in order to restore US credibility as a super power and to halt Soviet expansionism in southern Africa.

To meet the first challenge, Kissinger has continually insisted that "all Cuban forces must be withdrawn from the country before the United States extends diplomatic recognition to Angola."[158] To pressure the MPLA leaders, Kissinger has announced the US intention to block Angola's admission to the UN as long as Cuban troops remain in Angola. He has solicited the help of other African governments to convince Luanda to avoid a showdown in the UN by asking for a delay in its application for membership to the world body.

As for Rhodesia, Kissinger has announced that the United States is firmly committed to the principle of majority rule and has no intention of giving military assistance to the white-dominated regime of Ian Smith. Nevertheless, the Ford administration will not tolerate any

Cuban or Soviet intervention in Rhodesia. Kissinger has promised, "The United States would do all it could to bring about a change in Rhodesia."[159]

Some observers think that his Rhodesian policy is contradictory. They argue that Smith can now become more adamant, knowing that the US is in total opposition to any Communist intervention on the side of the African majority. Senator Dick Clark, Chairman of the Senate Foreign Relations Subcommittee on Africa, commented: "I think Kissinger and the administration are determined to take action against Cuba if the Cubans get involved again in a major way and that, if it comes, it will be action against Cuba itself."[160]

Kissinger contends that the two objectives can be accomplished simultaneously.[161] He has shown coolness in his relations with Moscow, for example by postponing some previously scheduled meetings with Russian officials, as an indication that Soviet-American relationships cannot be improved as long as Cuban forces remain in Angola. He has also told Smith not to interpret American opposition to possible Communist intervention as support of his regime and has renewed contacts with Britain in order to reinforce British pressure on Smith to grant majority rule.

The collapse of the Smith-Nkomo talks in March, 1976, accompanied by the escalation of guerrilla warfare inside Rhodesia, led Kissinger to travel to southern Africa in April in an attempt to avert the possibility of a wider racial war and to consult with African leaders on how the US could best help to solve African problems. Kissinger also hoped the trip would demonstrate the growing US interest in Africa, warn Cuba and the Soviet Union against further military ventures in the area and redirect US-southern African policy. In his Lusaka speech on April 27, Kissinger indicated the outlines of a new US policy (see Appendix B).

The new policy pays immediate attention to Rhodesia which, in Kissinger's view, is "the most urgent" problem. Kissinger outlined the administration stance on this issue in considerable detail in order to take the thunder out of the Soviet-Cuban presence in southern Africa, to give Smith clear signals on the US position and to boost British efforts to achieve majority rule through a negotiated settlement. He explicitly announced that the United States is "wholly committed to help bring about a rapid, just and African solution (in Rhodesia)." He even offered to act as an intermediary in future negotiations to secure a swift transition to black majority rule in Rhodesia. He promised that he would "urge the Congress this year to repeal the Byrd Amendment — which authorizes Rhodesian chrome imports to the United States — an act inconsistent with UN sanctions."[162]

In his policy statement, Kissinger drew a fine distinction between the problems of Rhodesia and Namibia on the one hand and South Africa on the other. He reiterated the well-publicized American position that South Africa is illegally occupying Namibia and called on Pretoria to set up a timetable for self-determination in that country under the supervision of the UN and with participation by African groups currently banned there. Kissinger, who must have been influenced by his private visit to Pretoria in the 1960s prior to joining the Nixon administration, believes that South Africans are "not colonialists; historically, they are an African people." He has insisted, however, that "the institutionalized separation of the races must end" and has promised to continue "to encourage and work for peaceful change."[163]

The new policy therefore continues to grant South Africa a special place in US strategy. This is evident in Kissinger's appeal to Pretoria to use "its influence in Salisbury to promote a rapid negotiated settlement for majority rule in Rhodesia."[164] South Africa is indeed the only country capable of applying effective pressure on the Smith regime because "with the closing of the border by Mozambique, South African roads and railways are now almost the only supports for the Rhodesian economy."[165] It is speculated that Prime Minister John Vorster might be tempted to intensify that pressure on Ian Smith in return for "credits and a degree of continental legitimacy from black Africa."[166] Kissinger believes that Pretoria's efforts in this direction will "show its dedication to Africa" and will be "viewed positively by the community of nations as well as by the rest of Africa."[167]

The main purpose of the new Ford-Kissinger policy is to find solutions to southern Africa's chronic racial and colonial problems that can be broadly satisfactory to African leaders but that also guarantee continued white rule in South Africa. If the new initiatives are successful, the US would not have to choose between Pretoria and Africa and would be able to maintain its fast growing investment ($1.5 billion in 1974) and its swelling trade surplus ($1.2 billion in exports and $609 million in imports during 1974) with South Africa. As *Fortune* magazine has pointed out, "South Africa has always been regarded by foreign investors as a gold mine, one of those rare and refreshing places where profits are great and problems small. Capital is not threatened by political instability or nationalization. Labor is cheap, the market booming, the currency hard and convertible."[168] This view helps explain the fact that US investment in South Africa accounts for 40 percent of all American investment in Africa. Since 1972, the level of investment has grown at a rate of 20 percent a year, despite the increased tension in the area. At present, approximately 50 percent of American investment is in manufacturing industries and another 33 percent is in machinery and chemicals. While the US Department of Commerce withholds information on investment in mining, petroleum and motor-vehicle production, most of the remaining 17 percent of total investment is in these areas. Overall, the US is the second largest investor in South Africa, holding 16 percent of total foreign investments there.[169]

Settlement of southern African problems could lead to greatly expanded business opportunities for Americans. US trade with the entire African continent is already much greater than its trade with South Africa (see Table 8). American firms would be able to increase their investments (currently estimated to be about $2.2 billion) in the developing countries of Africa and might even reverse the 6.5 percent decline in the total volume of American investment in 1974 that resulted from partial nationalization of oil companies in Nigeria. US investments are concentrated in petroleum ($1.3 billion) and mining and smelting ($446 million); together, these represent as much as 75 percent of total US investments in Africa.[170]

Africa is becoming increasingly important to the US because of the energy crisis and American dependence on Africa's oil and other mineral resources. Since 1972, for example, US imports of oil and raw materials have resulted in a large trade deficit with Africa. The deficit totalled $4 billion in 1975, $3 billion of which was accounted for by imports of Nigerian oil.[171]

If another NSSM document has been prepared by Kissinger for President Ford, it is most likely that supplies of natural resources have been extensively analyzed. The US is increasingly in need of many critical fuels and other minerals. This situation has led many observers to express concern over the growing demand for minerals, particularly in the second half of the 1970s. Anthony Harrigan remarked:

> The United States is not only facing an energy crisis in the mid- and late 1970s but a minerals crisis as well. Access to strategic minerals will be an increasingly serious national concern in the latter part of this decade. The same situation applies to NATO countries, of course.[172]

It is in this sector of resource scarcity that the importance of southern Africa must be considered. Trade figures reveal that the United States has already relied heavily on Africa to meet its mineral needs. Of the minerals imported from Africa — including chrome, platinum, manganese ore, cobalt, gold, diamonds and oil — most are taken from southern Africa. The US imports 47 percent of its chrome from South Africa and Rhodesia, for example. Of all the southern African countries, South Africa is the most important to the US. Indeed, South Africa alone accounted for 36 percent of chrome, 51 percent of vanadium, 31 percent of platinum and 14 percent of manganese imports by the US in 1975.[173]

In the midst of the mounting crisis in southern Africa, an extra-

Table 8
US Trade with Africa and South Africa (In millions of dollars)

	EXPORTS						IMPORTS					
	1960	1965	1970	1972	1973	1974	1960	1965	1970	1972	1973	1974
	793	1,229	1,580	1,577	2,306	3,659	534	878	1,113	1,595	2,583	6,617
Algeria	28	21	62	98	161	315	1	8	10	104	215	1,091
Angola	11	13	38	26	38	62	26	48	68	90	167	378
Cameroon, Federal Republic of	(x)	7	19	37	15	20	13	13	25	24	30	27
Central African Republic	(x)	1	1	1	3	1	(x)	10	6	7	8	7
Egypt	151	158	77	76	225	455	32	16	23	17	26	70
Ethiopia	12	22	26	24	25	33	27	64	67	58	79	64
Gabon	(x)	5	7	13	19	33	(x)	11	9	11	12	162
Ghana	17	36	59	44	63	77	52	59	91	80	90	126
Ivory Coast	(x)	11	36	22	69	49	(x)	46	92	92	108	95
Kenya	(x)	24	34	26	39	49	(x)	13	23	27	26	39
Liberia	36	39	46	41	46	70	39	51	51	52	72	96
Libya	43	65	108	85	104	139	(z)	30	39	116	216	1
Malagasy Republic	3	4	7	11	15	7	13	29	32	37	40	60
Mauritania	(x)	4	4	5	9	11	(x)	2	1	1	1	(z)
Morocco	36	56	89	58	113	184	10	6	10	11	14	20
Mozambique	10	9	22	16	32	32	5	7	18	26	34	45
Nigeria	26	74	129	114	161	286	40	60	71	271	652	3,286
*South Africa, Republic of	288	438	563	602	746	1,160	108	226	290	325	377	609
Sudan	7	15	7	18	39	64	5	7	12	12	9	27
Tanzania	(x)	7	12	12	11	51	(x)	11	24	21	27	26
Tunisia	22	44	49	55	60	87	(z)	2	3	8	33	21
Uganda	(x)	2	4	3	2	8	(x)	43	48	49	57	67
Zaire	(x)	71	62	37	110	145	(x)	38	41	43	71	68
Zambia	(x)	(x)	31	34	39	68	(x)	(x)	2	3	6	6
Other	103	103	89	119	163	253	174	77	59	110	213	226

X Not applicable.
Z Less than $500,000.
Source: US Department of Commerce, Bureau of Census, *Statistical Abstract of the United States*, July 1975.

ordinary report on South Africa's strategic mineral importance has appeared in England. On March 22, 1976, the *Guardian's* science correspondent noted:

> Behind the battles for political power in central and south Africa lie the resources on which the future of technology in the industralized world depends. The energy future of the world in the post-oil era now seems likely to rest on lithium and, outside the United States, by far the largest known deposits in the Western world lie in Rhodesia and South Africa.[174]

It is expected that lithium will be used in high-power batteries and in fusion. The former is viewed as the key to the enormous transformation of vehicles from oil to electric power. In terms of fusion, demand for lithium will be even greater since pressure is expected to grow for "clean" nuclear fusion based on use of lithium, rather than "dirty" plutonium bred in fast reactors. In spite of large American deposits, the US will probably be able to meet only a portion of its requirements for lithium.

This report concerning possible lithium scarcities complements the warnings contained in a recent study by the US Geological Survey. It asserted:

> The United States could face problems in trying to increase its domestic energy resources because it lacks sufficient supplies of some of the minerals necessary for such development . . . . The fear that other countries may form cartels for the needed substances — as the oil exporters have done — was a factor that prompted the study.[175]

The study mentions that the US could face particularly vulnerable shortages of manganese, chromium, cobalt, titanium, mica and niobium. Besides the fact that South Africa possesses sizable reserves of almost all the base metals and metallic minerals, its reliability as a dependable source has been noted by the US government. A strategic minerals study published in November, 1974, by the White House Office on International Economic Affairs stated:

> Canada, Australia or South Africa would be unlikely to participate in any embargo of exports to the United States, Western Europe or Japan. Since these countries are the most important sources of raw materials for the United States . . . any embargo threat for commodities is greatly diminished.[176]

As the US and other industrialized countries increasingly develop nuclear energy programs, South Africa — possessing 25 percent of the world's uranium reserves — has the potential for emerging as a "nuclear energy exporting power." As L. Alberts, President of South Africa's Atomic Energy Board, stated frankly: "We now have a bargaining position equal to that of any Arab country with a lot of oil."[177] The OECD recently estimated that South African uranium production could increase by more than four times by 1985[178] It is also predicted that South Africa's own nuclear capacity will increase seven-fold in the next decade.[179] Beginning with a nuclear reactor originally supplied under the Atoms for Peace program, South Africa bought two large computers from the US in 1973 that are now being used to run a secret uranium enrichment plant at Pelindaba in South Africa.[180] Because Pretoria has not signed the nuclear non-proliferation treaty, this means that South Africa has been "using the computers in a facility outside UN jurisdiction;" it is also possible that it could use them "to expand its enrichment plant to make uranium for atomic weapons instead of electricity."[181] Furthermore, General Electric has just applied for a license to sell South Africa two huge atomic power plants. Given its growing nuclear power, South Africa will have ample technology and materiel to produce a sizable nuclear weapons arsenal.

The broad confluence of strategic thinking and beneficial economic cooperation has brought Washington and Pretoria closer to each other. The Ford administration would like to defuse the escalating tension in southern Africa and to assist South Africa to normalize relations with the rest of Africa. Kissinger's strategy is to end the Rhodesian conflict, to promise independence for Namibia and to remove racial restrictions under apartheid in order to enhance South Africa's detente with Zambia, Zaire and the Ivory Coast as well as to preserve Pretoria's dominance in southern Africa. Because of its mineral wealth and politico-military power, South Africa is likely to continue to occupy a central place in US-southern African policy.

The future of the new Ford-Kissinger policy is uncertain in a year that is filled with Presidential primaries and an election in the fall. The program has already run into opposition because some Republican leaders think that the new African policy cost President Ford critical votes in the Presidential primaries in Texas, Alabama, Georgia and Indiana. They have advised the President to delay the implementation of such a policy until after the November election. Senate Majority Whip Robert C. Byrd (D — West Virginia) and Senator James B. Allen (D — Alabama) have threatened to filibuster to remove the $25 million earmarked for black-ruled nations from the total request for aid to southern Africa that is needed to help carry out the pledges made by Kissinger during his African visit. Allen has objected to giving economic assistance to African states bordering Rhodesia, particularly "communist-controlled Mozambique," believing the aid could "persuade them to join in the battle against the stable government in Rhodesia."[182] Republican Presidential candidate Ronald Reagan has joined the bandwagon in criticizing Kissinger's African policy of "aiding black Africa while at the same time seeking to press for an end to the white-minority-ruled government in Rhodesia."[183]

President Ford has become more sensitive to this criticism and has avoided taking a position on additional economic assistance to southern Africa. From all indications, it seems that the future US course in southern Africa will not become clear until after the Presidential election in the fall. Whether Kissinger's newly initiated policy will be partially or totally carried out will largely depend on who the President will be for the next four years. If Ford is elected, the chances for implementing such a policy will be much greater. However, a new President in the White House might have his own views on the kind of policy he wants to see in southern Africa.

(remarks excerpted from seminar, University of California, 1968.)

FOOTNOTES

1. Donald B. Easum, "United States Policy Toward Africa," *Issue* 5:3, 1975, pp. 70-71.
2. Donald F. McHenry, "Statement on South Africa and Namibia," *Ibid.*, p. 60.
3. US, National Security Council Interdepartmental Group for Africa. Study in Response to National Security Memorandum 39: Southern Africa. Washington, DC: National Security Council, August 15, 1969, p. 86. Hereafter referred to as NSSM 39 (1969).
4. Mohamed El-Khawas, "Kissinger on Africa: Benign Neglect?" *A Current Bibliography on African Affairs,* 7:1, 1974, p. 3.
5. *The Washington Post*, Sept. 17, 1973 (remarks excerpted from seminar, University of California, 1968.)
6. Memorandum by Henry A. Kissinger to Secretaries of State and Defense and CIA Director, April 10, 1969. (NSSM 39).
7. Edgar Lockwood, "National Security Memorandum 39 and the Future of United States Policy toward Southern Africa," *Issue*, 4:3, 1974, p. 63.
8. NSSM 39, pp. 86-88.
9. *Ibid.*, p. 93.
10. *Ibid.*, p. 101.
11. *Ibid.*, p. 86.
12. Mohamed A. El-Khawas, "United States Foreign Policy Toward Africa, 1960-1972," *A Current Bibliography on African Affairs*, 5:2, 1972, p. 412.
13. NSSM 39, p. 103.
14. John Seiler, "The Future of US-Southern African Policy," *Issue*, 2:1, 1972, pp. 21-22.
15. NSSM 39, p. 111.
16. McHenry, p. 60.
17. NSSM, p. 117.
18. *Ibid.*, p. 107.
19. McHenry, p. 61.
20. John A. Marcum, *The Politics of Indifference: Portugal and Africa, A Case Study in American Foreign Policy.* Syracuse, New York: Syracuse University Press, Eastern African Studies V, March 1972, pp. 23-24. See also Henry A. Kissinger, *The Troubled Partnership: A Reappraisal of the Atlantic Alliance.* New York: McGraw-Hill, 1965, p. 205.
21. NSSM 39, p. 87.
22. *Ibid.*, p. 105.
23. *Ibid.*
24. Willard R. Johnson, "United States Foreign Policy Toward Africa," *Africa Today*, 20:1, 1973, p. 22.
25. *The Washington Post*, Sept. 12, 1973.
26. *Ibid.*
27. *ITT-CIA Subversion in Chile: A Case Study of US Corporate Intrigue in the Third World.* Nottingham, England: Spokesman Books, 1972.
28. Immanuel Wallerstein, "From Nixon to Nixon," *Africa Report*, 14:8, 1969, p. 30.
29. NSSM 39, p. 105.
30. *Ibid.*
31. McHenry, p. 61.
32. Lockwood, *NSSM 39 . . .*, p. 63.
33. *Ibid.*, p. 67.

34. George M. Houser, *United States Policy and Southern Africa*. New York: The Africa Fund (American Committee on Africa), 1974, p. 5.

35. *The Johannesburg Star*, January 5, 1974.

36. "Employment Practices of US Firms in South Africa." Washington, DC: Department of State, Bureau of African Affairs, February 1973.

37. Marilyn Berger, "Loan to South Africa is Guaranteed by US," *The Washington Post*, January 15, 1972; *US Policy Toward Southern Africa*, Hearings, Subcommittee on African Affairs of the Committee on Foreign Relations, United States Senate, July 24, 1975. Washington, DC: Government Printing Office, 1976, p. 351.

38. US Chamber of Commerce, *Survey of Current Business*, 1969-1974, Washington, DC, yearly issues.

39. US Department of Commerce, Bureau of Census. *Statistical Abstract of the United States, 1975*. Washington, DC: Government Printing Office, 1975. For data on US exports to and imports from South Africa in 1968, see NSSM 39, p. 87.

40. *Survey of Current Business*, 1968-1974.

41. Easum, p. 68.

42. Mohamed A. El-Khawas, "A Perspective on US Investment in South Africa," in *Impact: US Constituency for Africa*. Published by the Washington Task Force on African Affairs, 1973, p. 10; Reed Kramer and Tami Hultman, "The Impact of US Investment in Southern Africa," *Social Action*, 38:7, 1972, pp. 4-11; *Southern Africa: Proposals for Americans*. A Report by the UN Association of the USA. New York, December 1971, pp. 29-30.

43. Easum, p. 68.

44. Baden Hickman, "Call to Halt Funds for South Africa," *Guardian*, March 10, 1976.

45. See *The Energy Crisis and US Foreign Policy*. Washington, DC: Overseas Development Council, Development Paper 14, August 1973; and *Special Report: Critical Imported Materials*. Washington, DC: Council on International Economic Policy, December 1974; "Material Needs and the Environment, Today and Tomorrow." Washington, DC: National Commission on Material Policy, June 1973.

46. US Dept. of State, African Affairs Advisory Council. *Africa's Resources*. Washington, DC: US Dept. of State, August 1971, p. 1.

47. *Ibid.*, pp. 4, 8.

48. *Ibid.*, pp. 6, 8, 13-15, 21.

49. NSSM 39, p. 107.

50. Bruce Oudes, "South Africa, US Secrets," *The Sun*, February 22, 1976.

51. *Implementation of the US Arms Embargo*, Hearings of the Subcommittee on Africa, House Committee on African Affairs, 93rd Congress, 1st session, March 20, 22 and April 6, 1973. Washington, DC; US Government Printing Office, 1973, pp. 42, 59.

52. *Ibid.*, p. 55.

53. *Ibid.*, p. 59.

54. Houser, p. 5.

55. Ernest Harsch and Tony Thomas. *Angola: The Hidden History of Washington's War*. New York: Pathfinder Press, Inc., 1976, p. 117.

56. NSSM 39, p. 122.

57. Goler Butcher, "Testimony on South Africa and US Foreign Policy," *Issue*, 5:3, 1975, p. 42.

58. NSSM 39, pp. 122-123.

59. *Anti-Apartheid News*. London, England, November 1973.

60. "The Drift Towards NATO Intervention in Southern Africa," *Southern Africa*, December, 1974, pp. 4-5; Easum, p. 70.
61. Tad Szulc, "Why are We in Johannesburg?" *Esquire*, October 1974, p. 48.
62. *The Wall Street Journal*, July 31, 1975.
63. "NATO Arms, South Africa," *Africa*, July 1975, pp. 34-35.
64. "The Indian Ocean and Africa," *Africa Confidential*, August 29, 1974, p. 26.
65. Earl W. Foell, "Africa's Vanishing Act at the UN: Where Does the United States Stand on African Issues?" *Africa Report*, 14:8, 1969, p. 31; see also El-Khawas, "United States . . .," p. 415.
66. Bruce Oudes, "Dialog: Was Rogers' African Tour a Bad Trip?" *Africa Report*, 15:4, 1970, pp. 22-24.
67. NSSM 39, p. 106.
68. Edgar Lockwood, "Testimony on Rhodesia and United States Foreign Policy," *Issue*, 5:3, 1975, p. 25.
69. NSSM 39, Annex 4, p. 150.
70. *US Policy Toward Southern Africa*, Hearing of the Subcommittee on African Affairs, *op. cit.*, June-July 1975, p. 4.
71. Statements made by Reps. Ronald V. Dellums (D – California), Jonathan B. Bingham (D – New York) and Donald M. Fraser (D – Minnesota), US Congressional Record, Proceeding and Debates of the 92nd Congress, First Session. November 10, 1971, H. 10859-63.
72. *Ibid.*, H. 10860.
73. *Ibid.*, H 10859.
74. *Ibid.*, H. 10860.
75. *Rhodesian Chrome*. A Research Report by the Washington Intern Program of the Student and Young Adult Division. New York: United Nations Association of the USA, May 1973, p. 43.
76. "Richard M. Nixon: An Interview with his Spokesman, David D. Newsom," *Africa Report*, 17:3, 1972, p. 15.
77. Seiler, p. 21.
78. *Rhodesian Chrome*, p. 37.
79. *Ibid.*
80. Ken Owen, "Why Nixon Took Option 2," *The Johannesburg Star*, February 13, 1971.
81. *The New York Times*, April 21, 1971.
82. US Congressional Record, Proceedings and Debates of the 94th Congress, First Session, September 25, 1975, H. 9109.
83. *The Washington Post*, February 3, 1972.
84. *The Johannesburg Star*, September 8, 1973; *Africa Briefing International*, October 20, 1972.
85. *Rhodesian Chrome*, p. 41.
86. *The New York Times*, June 7, 1972.
87. Statement made by Rep. Wayne L. Hayes (D – Ohio), Congressional Record, Nov. 10, 1971, H. 10864; Mohamed A. El-Khawas, "Congressional Voting on African Issues: A Preliminary Assessment," in *Congress and Africa*. Washington, DC: African Bibliographic Center, Current Reading List Series, 10:1, 1973, pp. 7-8.
88. The Washington Office on Africa. *Legislative Bulletin*, August 18, 1972, p. 2.
89. *US Policy Toward Southern Africa*, Hearings . . ., June-July 1975, p. 185.
90. NSSM 39, Annex 3, p. 145.
91. *Ibid.*
92. Lockwood, "Testimony on Rhodesia . . ., " p. 25.

93. *Ibid.*, pp. 26-27.

94. Jean Herskovits, "An Overview of American and African Policies in Regard to Southern Africa," *Issue*, 5:3, 1975, p. 52; Barbara Rogers, "Congress and Southern Africa," *A Current Bibliography on African Affairs*, 7:1, 1974, p. 28.

95. Jose Sherclif, "Portugal's Strategic Territories," *Foreign Affairs*, 31:2, 1953, pp. 321-25.

96. David M. Abshire, "Strategic Implications," in *Portuguese Africa: A Handbook*. Edited by David M. Abshire and Michael A. Samuels. New York: Praeger, 1969, pp. 435, 436.

97. Mohamed A. El-Khawas, "American Involvement in Portuguese Africa: The Legacy of the Nixon Years," *UFAHAMU*, 6:1, 1975, p. 118.

98. NSSM 39, p. 108.

99. *Ibid.*, p. 107.

100. Jack Anderson, "State Resisted Kissinger's African Policy," *The Washington Post*, October 22, 1974; "Henry Kissinger's First Big Tilt," *Ibid.*, October 11, 1974.

101. Johnson, pp. 20-21.

102. *The Economist*, October 6, 1973, p. 38.

103. *US Business Involvement in Southern Africa: Part I.* Hearings of the Subcommittee on Africa, House Committee on Foreign Affairs, 92nd Congress, 1st Session, May 4, 5, 11, 12, June 2, 3, 15, 16, 30, and July 15, 1971. Washington, DC: US Government Printing Office, 1972, p. 286.

104. *Ibid.*

105. Marcello Caetano, *Guidelines of Foreign Policy*. Lisbon: Secretaria de Estado do Informacao e Tourismo, 1970, p. 7.

106. Marcum, *The Politics of Indifference . . .*, p. 23.

107. US Dept. of State Bulletin, 66:1697, January 3, 1972, pp. 54-5.

108. El-Khawas, "Kissinger . . .," p. 6.

109. *The Washington Post*, October 13, 1974.

110. *Implementation of the US Arms Embargo*. Hearings . . ., pp. 52, 58, and 61.

111. US Dept. of Commerce, Bureau of International Commerce. *Foreign Economic Trends and their Implications for the US*, October 1969, p. 9 and August 1972, p. 8.

112. Supplementary Working Paper prepared by the UN Secretariat for the members of Subcommittee 1, Special Committee, Conference Room Paper SC 1/73/1, June 12, 1973, p. 6.

113. *Ibid.*, pp. 11-26.

114. Mohamed A. El-Khawas, "Foreign Economic Involvement in Angola and Mozambique," *Issue*, 4:2, 1974, pp. 23-25.

115. *Ibid.*, pp. 25-26; UN Subcommittee 1, Special Committee, Conference Room Paper SC.1/73/2, June 8, 1973, pp. 10-15.

116. UNA/USA, *Southern Africa*, pp. 69-70.

117. *The Washington Star-News*, October 9, 1974.

118. Richard M. Nixon, "US Foreign Policy for the 1970s: Shaping a Durable Peace." A Report to Congress, May 3, 1973. Washington, DC: US Government Printing Office, 1973, p. 159.

119. *The Johannesburg Star*, March 8, 1975.

120. *Southern Africa*, July-August, 1975, p. 37.

121. Maxine Isaacs Burns, "Visitors to Pretoria," *Africa Report*, 20:5, 1975, pp. 49-50.

122. Robert Manning, "L'Offensive Sud-Africaine," *Le Monde Diplomatique*, February 1976, p. 14; *The Johannesburg Star*, May 24, 1975.

123. *The Washington Post*, November 29, 1974.
124. *US Policy Toward Southern Africa*, Hearings . . ., p. 343.
125. David B. Ottaway, "South Africa Cheered by US Move," *The Washington Post*, June 5, 1975.
126. "Ford Favors Rhodesian Chrome Ban," *Ibid.*, August 21, 1974; Leslie H. Gelb, "Ford Acts to Bar Rhodesian Chrome," *The New York Times*, August 21, 1974.
127. Edgar Lockwood, "An Inside Look at the Sanctions Campaign," *Issue*, 4:3, 1974, pp. 73-74.
128. *Congressional Record*, September 25, 1975, H. 9107.
129. The Washington Office on Africa. *Washington Notes on Africa*, October 1975, p. 3.
130. *Ibid.*, pp. 2-3.
131. Congressional Record, September 25, 1975, H. 9111.
132. *Ibid.*, H. 9106, 9107.
133. "Text of Kissinger's Address in Zambia on US Policy Toward Southern Africa," *The New York Times*, April 28, 1976.
134. Allen Isaacman, "Mozambique and the United States: A Decade of Struggle and a Year of Decision", *Issue*, 5:3, 1975, p. 8.
135. *Ibid.*
136. *Ibid.*, pp. 7-8.
137. Henry A. Kissinger, "Building an Enduring Foreign Policy," Speech before the Economic Club of Detroit, Michigan, 24 November 1975. Washington, DC: US Dept. of State, Bureau of Public Affairs, 1975, p. 3.
138. David S. Broder, "[Ford] Assails Senate for Aid Slash," *The Washington Post*, December 31, 1975.
139. Murray Marder, "The Angola Involvement: US, Soviets Caught in a Byzantine Conflict," *Ibid.*, January 6, 1976.
140. *Ibid.*
141. Mohamed A. El-Khawas, "Power Struggle in Angola: Who's Struggle? Who's Power?," Paper presented at the Southeastern Regional Seminar in African Studies at the University of Virginia, Charlottesville, April 17, 1976, p. 8.
142. Drew Middleton, "Soviet Aid Goal: Bases in Angola," *The Washington Star*, November 28, 1975.
143. David Binder, "US Reported Giving Angolan Anti-Reds $50 Million in Arms Aid," *The New York Times*, December 12, 1975.
144. Henry Kamm, "South Africans Said to Pull Out," *Ibid.*, January 26, 1976.
145. *The Washington Post,* January 28, 1976.
146. Carl T. Rowan, "Kissinger Threats Are Not an African Policy," *The Washington Star*, March 26, 1976.
147. *The Washington Post*, December 15, 1975.
148. "South Africa and the World," *Africa Today*, 23:1, 1976, p. 9.
149. Szulc, p. 48. See also Roger Morris, "The Proxy War in Angola: Pathology of a blunder," The New Republic, January 31, 1976, p. 22.
150. *The New York Times*, February 5, 1976.
151. Robert Keatley, "Black-Rule Movement Is Spreading in Africa, Putting US on Spot," *The Wall Street Journal*, March 23, 1976.
152. *The Christian Science Monitor*, March 24, 1976; *The Washington Post*, May 21, 1976.
153. *The New York Times*, March 29, 1976.
154. *Ibid.*
155. *The Christian Science Monitor*, March 29, 1976.

156. *The Washington Post*, March 28, 1976.
157. *The Christian Science Monitor*, March 29, 1976.
158. *The Washington Post*, May 25, 1976.
159. *The New York Times*, March 27, 1976.
160. Dana Adams Schmidt, "Kissinger Warns Cuba on Africa," *The Christian Science Monitor*, March 24, 1976.
161. *The Sun*, March 27, 1976.
162. "Southern Africa and the United States: An Agenda for Cooperation," Speech delivered by Secretary Henry A. Kissinger in Lusaka, Zambia, April 27, 1976 (see Appendix B).
163. *Ibid.*
164. *Ibid.*
165. Michael T. Kaufman, "The Kissinger Mission in Africa," *The New York Times*, April 30, 1976.
166. *Ibid.*
167. Appendix B.
168. John Blashill, "The Proper Role of US Corporations in South Africa," *Fortune*, July 1972, p. 49.
169. Paul Lewis, "Billion-Dollar Stakes in Africa," *The New York Times*, May 9, 1976.
170. *Ibid.*
171. *Ibid.*
172. Anthony Harrigan, "Security Interests in the Persian Gulf and Western Indian Ocean," *Strategic Review*, Fall 1973, p. 19.
173. *The New York Times*, May 9, 1976.
174. Anthony Tucker, "Power on Deposit," *Guardian*, March 22, 1976.
175. Sara Hansard, "Mineral Shortage Stirs Fear on US Energy Development," *International Herald Tribune*, January 14, 1976.
176. *Southern Africa*, April 1975, p. 7.
177. *Africa News*, April 10, 1975.
178. *The Johannesburg Star Weekly*, March 20, 1976.
179. Manning, p. 14.
180. *The Washington Post*, May 26, 1976.
181. *Ibid.*
182. *Ibid.*, May 25, 1976.
183. *The Washington Star*, May 26, 1976.

PART II

**National Security
Study Memorandum 39
(The Kissinger Study of Southern Africa)**

April 10, 1969

National Security Study Memorandum 39

TO: The Secretary of State
             The Secretary of Defense
             Director, Central Intelligence Agency

SUBJECT: Southern Africa

     The President has directed a comprehensive review of U.S. policy toward Southern Africa (south of Congo (K) and Tanzania).

     The study should consider (1) the background and future prospects of major problems in the area; (2) alternative views of the U.S. interest in Southern Africa; and (3) the full range of basic strategies and policy options open to the United States.

     The review of interests and policy options should encompass the area as a whole -- including Southern Rhodesia, South Africa, the Portuguese territories, and adjacent African states.

     The President has directed that the NSC Interdepartmental Group for Africa perform this study.

     The study should be forwarded to the NSC Review Group by April 25th.

Henry A. Kissinger

cc: Secretary of the Treasury
    Secretary of Commerce
    Chairman, Joint Chiefs of Staff
    Administrator, AID
    Acting Director, NASA

NATIONAL SECURITY COUNCIL
INTERDEPARTMENTAL GROUP FOR AFRICA

Study in Response to National Security Study
Memorandum 39:

Southern Africa

(SECRET)

(SECRET)

NATIONAL SECURITY COUNCIL
INTERDEPARTMENTAL GROUP FOR AFRICA

Study in Response to National Security Study
Memorandum 39:

Southern Africa

Table of Contents

1. SUMMARY

A. The Area

The black states of Zambia, Malawi, Swaziland, Lesotho and Botswana. The white minority
area of South Africa, South West Africa, Southern Rhodesia, Mozambique and Angola. Tanzania,
while not in the area designated, is closely
linked to the problem.

B. The Problem (pp. 117-119)

Racial repression by white minority regimes
and the black African opposition to it pose two
problems for US interest in the area:

1. Our interests in the white states to the
degree they are seen as at least tacit acceptance of racism affect our standing with
African and other states.
2. The prospect of increasing violence in the
area growing out of black insurgency and white
reprisal could jeopardize our interests in the
future.

Our interests in the region are important
but not vital. Our investments, primarily in
South Africa, total about $1 billion and our
trade yields a highly favorable balance of payments advantage. This geographically important
area has major ship repair and logistics facilities which can be useful to our defense forces.
An important NASA space tracking station is
located in South Africa. Outside of the region
our investments in Africa total about $1.5 bil-
lion and profitable trade relations are expanding. Relationships involving these economic
interests and a variety of other matters in-

cluding US defense installations, elsewhere in
Africa could become more difficult if our policies in southern Africa generate intense adverse
reaction.

In the United Nations, the US has firmly opposed the racial and colonial policies of the
white regimes. The Afro-Asian states, however,
have steadily increased their demands for
stronger UN measures including sanctions and the
use of force to give effect to UN actions. The
US has resisted these demands. While the Soviet
Union and China do not accord southern Africa a
high priority, they have taken firm positions
supporting the liberation goals of the blacks
and given some support to the liberation movements. In so doing, they have made some gains
in Africa and in the UN.

C. US Objectives (page 101)

There are several broad objectives of US
policy towards southern Africa. Arranged without intent to imply priority, they are:

- to improve the US standing in black Africa
  and internationally on the racial issue.
- to minimize the likelihood of escalation of
  violence in the area and risk of US involvement.
- to minimize the opportunities for the USSR
  and Communist China to exploit the racial
  issue in the region for propaganda advantage
  and to gain political influence with black
  governments and liberation movements.
- to encourage moderation of the current rigid
  racial and colonial policies of the white
  regimes.
- to protect economic, scientific and strategic
  interests and opportunities in the region, including the orderly marketing of South
  Africa's gold production.

These objectives in some instances are conflicting and irreconcilable. Moreover, views of
priority vary widely, depending primarily upon
the perception of the nature of the problems in
the area and US interests.

D. The Policy Dilemma within the US
    Government (pp. 89-92)

There is agreement that:

1. The US does not have vital security interests in the region.
2. The racial policies of the white regime
states have become a major international
issue in the post-colonial world and accordingly US foreign policy must take them into
account.
3. The racial problems of southern Africa
probably will become more acute, perhaps
leading to major violence and greater involvement of the communist powers.

There is disagreement over:

1. Whether there is any prospect for non-
violent change.
2. Whether any external influence or internal
development can induce either side to moderate its position on the racial and colonial
issues of the area.
3. The extent to which pursuit of our tangible interests in the white states is likely
to do appreciable damage to our present or
long term political and other interests in
the black states of the region, in the rest
of Africa, or elsewhere, including the UN.

E. The Range of Choice (pp. 101-103)

The general policy question centers on US
posture toward the white regimes -- a key element in our relations with the black states in
the area and a factor of varying degree of importance throughout the continent.
But the range of feasible policy options is
limited. On one extreme our interests do not
justify consideration of US military intervention in the area. Similarly economic sanctions
against Portugal or South Africa are excluded
both because they are likely to be ineffective
and because they could lead to a US military
involvement in their enforcement. On the other

extreme we cannot accept or endorse either the
racial or colonial policies of the white regimes. Nor can we identify ourselves with violent or repressive solutions to the area's
problems on either side of the confrontation.

F. The Options

   Option One (pp. 103-105): Closer association
with the white regimes to protect and enhance
our economic, strategic and scientific interests.

   Premise: Our disagreement with the domestic
policies of either side should not inhibit our
relations with them. We can have no significant
effect on the situation in the region. Therefore
we should pursue our economic, strategic and
scientific interests because the political costs
will not be excessive.

   Options Two (pp. 105-109): Broader association
with both black and white states in an effort
to encourage moderation in the white states, to
enlist cooperation of the black states in reducing tensions and the likelihood of increasing
cross-border violence, and to encourage improved
relations among states in area.

   Premise: The blacks cannot gain political
rights through violence. Constructive change can
come only by acquiescence of the whites. We can
by selective relaxation of our stance toward the
white states and increased economic assistance to
the black states in the region help to draw the
groups together. Our tangible interests are a
basis for contacts in the region and can be
maintained at acceptable political costs.

   Option Three (pp. 109-111): Limited association
with the white states and continuing association
with blacks in an effort to retain some economic, scientific, and strategic interest in the
white states while maintaining a posture on the
racial issue which the blacks will accept,
though opposing violent solutions to the problems of the region.

Premise: We cannot significantly influence
the domestic policies of the white states; nor
is there any internal indication of change.
Maintenance of a posture on the racial question
acceptable to the black states of the region and
elsewhere need not entail giving up all material
interests in the white states.

Option Four (pp. 111-114): Dissociation from
the white regimes with closer relations with the
black states in an effort to enhance our standing on the racial issue in Africa and internationally.

Premise: We cannot influence the white states
for constructive change and therefore increasing
violence is likely. Only by cutting our ties
with the white regimes can we protect our standing on the race issue in black Africa and internationally. Since our tangible interests are not
vital, this is a reasonable price to pay.

Option Five (pp. 114-116): Dissociation from
both black and white states in an effort to
limit our involvement in the problems of the
area.

Premise: The racial confrontation in southern
Africa is unmanageable and potentially dangerous
and will grow worse despite any effort we might
make. Thus we should lower our profile in the
area and avoid identification with either side.

(See pp. 103-116 for a fuller description of
the options, including illustrative courses of
action and the pros and cons.)

II. A. US INTERESTS IN SOUTHERN AFRICA

Our Policy positions on southern African issues
affect a range of US interests. None of the interests are vital to our security, but they have
political and material importance. Some of these
interests are concrete and evident in the region
itself, while others relate to our position in
black Africa and the world. The interests can be
summarized as follows:

1. Political

Racial repression by white minority regimes
in southern Africa has international political
ramifications extending beyond the region itself. Politically conscious blacks elsewhere in
Africa and the world deeply resent the continuation of discrimination, identify with the
repressed majorities in southern Africa and
tend in varying degrees to see relationships of
outside powers with the white regimes as at
least tacit acceptance of racism. Many others
in the non-white world tend to share this view
in some measure. The communist states have been
quick to seize on this issue and to support
black aspirations. Thus our policy toward the
white regimes of southern Africa affects, though
it may not necessarily govern, our standing with
African and other states on issues in the United
Nations and bilaterally. Depending on its intensity, adverse reaction to our policy in southern
Africa could make more difficult our reation-
ships elsewhere in Africa on a variety of matters including US defense installations, overflight rights and the use of port facilities.
The same consideration applies to economic relations: direct investment in Africa outside the
white regime states currently totals about $1.5

billion (of which the greater part is in black Africa south of the Sahara), or about two-thirds of the total US investment in Africa. US exports split about 60 percent in the black states of Africa and 40 percent in the white regime countries.

Because of the multiracial character of our society and our own racial problems, other countries tend to see our relationships with southern Africa as reflections of domestic attitudes on race. This situation is exacerbated by the extension of South Africa racial discrimination to black Americans who may be refused visas or who are subjected to segregated facilities in South Africa.

If violence in the area escalates, US interest will be increasingly threatened. In these circumstances the US would find it increasingly difficult without sacrificing interests to find a middle ground in the UN on questions of insurgent violence and counter-violence in the region and to resist demands for more positive actions against the white regimes.

2. Economic

US direct investment in southern Africa, mainly in South Africa, is about $1 billion and yields a highly profitable return. Trade, again mainly with South Africa, runs a favorable balance to the US (Our exports to South Africa were about $450 million in 1968 against imports of $250 million.) In addition, the US has indirect economic interest in the key role which South Africa plays in the UK balance of payments. UK investment in South Africa is currently estimated at $3 billion, and the British have made it clear that they will take no action which would jeopardize their economic interests. The US has an important interest in the orderly marketing of South Africa's gold production which is important to the successful operation of the two-tier gold price system.

3. Defense

Southern Africa is geographically important

for the US and its allies, particularly with the
closing of the Suez Canal and the increased
Soviet activity in the Indian Ocean. The US uses
overflight and landing facilities for military
aircraft in the Portuguese Territories and South
Africa. There are major ship repair and logistic
facilities in South Africa with a level of technical competence which cannot be duplicated elsewhere on the African continent. We have not
permitted US naval vessels to use South African
port facilities since early 1967, except for
emergencies. Regular use is made of ports in
Angola and Mozambique, however, but these ports
cannot accommodate aircraft carriers. The DOD
has a missile tracking station in South Africa
under a classified agreement and some of the
military aircraft traffic involves support of
this station. The future need for the DOD station is under review. The tentative conclusions
are that the station is no longer required for
research and development of missiles. We also
finance a UK atmosphere testing station for
nuclear materials located in Swaziland which
helps us monitor nuclear atmospheric explosions
worldwide.

4. Scientific

NASA has a space tracking facility of major
importance in South Africa, and overflight and
landing rights for support aircraft are utilized
in connection with various space shots. The NASA
station is particularly oriented towards support
of unmanned spacecraft and will be of key significance for planetary missions. We have an
atomic energy agreement with South Africa in-
itated under the Atoms for Peace program; this
relationship is important in influencing South
Africa to continue its policy of doing nothing
in the marketing of its large production of
uranium oxide which would have the effect of
increasing the number of nuclear weapons powers.

B. VIEWS OF THE US INTEREST IN SOUTHERN AFRICA

In weighing the range of US interest in southern Africa, there is basic consensus within the US government:

1. Although the US has various interests in the region, it has none which could be classified as vital security interests.
2. Our political interests in the region are important because the racial policies of the white states have become a major international issue. Therefore, because other countries have made it so, our foreign policy must take into account the domestic policies of the white regimes. Most non-white nations in the world in varying degrees would tend to judge conspicuous US cooperation with the white regimes as condoning their racial policies.
3. The racial problems of southern Africa probably will grow more acute over time, perhaps leading to violent internal upheavals and greater involvement of the communists powers. Though these developments may be years or even decades ahead, US policy should take account now of the risks to our interests and possible involvement over this uncertain future.

There are specific differences of view within the government regarding future trends in southern Africa and the US role in the area. These contrasting views are central to a judgment of US policy options. The following reflect a basic intellectual disagreement within the government in approaching the southern African problem:

89

1. Violent Change vs. Peaceful Evolution

Violent Change: Some argue that mounting
violence is inevitable unless change occurs and
that there is no prospect for peaceful change in
the racial policies of the white regimes, em-
bedded as they are in prejudice, religious
doctrine and self-interest and bolstered by economic prosperity, particularly in South Africa.
The results will be (a) black guerrilla and
terrorist activity on a growing scale within
these countries until change occurs, and (b) because of their support of the blacks, the Soviets
and Chinese will become the major beneficiaries
of the conflict.

Peaceful Evolution: Others contend that there
will be violence up to a point, since change can
only come slowly. But there is some prospect for
peaceful change in the white states in response
to internal economic and social forces. In any
event, peaceful evolution is the only avenue to
change because (a) black violence only produces
internal reaction, and (b) military realities
rule out a black victory at any stage. Moreover,
there are reasons to question the depth and
permanence of black resolve. Recently there has
been a decline in the level of insurgency. Neighboring black states - vital to successful guerrilla activity - will choose to preserve their
own security in the face of inevitable punishing
white retaliation at an early stage of any
significant guerrilla warfare.

2. The Possibility of US Influence Toward Peaceful Change

No influence: Some contend that we can
neither reform the whites nor restrain the
blacks. Racial repression is deeply ingrained
in the whites - the product of tradition, economic privilege and fears for their survival.
These attitudes are not amenable to the kinds
of influence one nation experts upon another
through peaceful international relations. Only
isolation and stronger forms of pressure (i.e.

90

force or mandatory economic sanctions backed by blockade) could have any impact.

Yet, they argue, without some change in the whites we cannot hope to influence the blacks to accept "peaceful evolution" as a substitute for force. The blacks will see such advice as a fundamental US betrayal of their cause.

A related school of thought believes that in this sensitive area any effort by the US to exert influence on internal policies could retard rather than stimulate the natural dynamics of change in the white-dominated societies.

Some Influence: Others argue that our tactical encouragement of economic and social forces already at work within the white regimes can constitute marginal but important influence for change. That influence, however, can be exerted only subtly and over several years. We should not give up whatever chance we have - through contacts with whites as well as blacks - to defuse the dangerous tensions in the area and to demonstrate the alternatives to the disastrous racial policies of the white regimes. Exposure of these regimes to the outside world is necessary if there is to be peaceful change. Isolation of the white societies has only intensified repressive policies. Moreover, external efforts to force change by pressure or coercion have unified the whites and produced an obdurate counter-reaction.

3. Importance of Political vs. Other Tangible Interests

Political Interests: Some argue that racial hostility as a reaction to centuries of white predominance is a relatively new political force in the world, gaining power and effectiveness as the developing countries become independent and control access to their own territories. We cannot foresee exactly when race will become a major factor in the international power balance, but that time is coming. It is equally clear that the racial repression by the white regimes in southern Africa is now the most volatile racial problem on the international scene.

91

For the non-white states, they also argue, the reckoning of support on the racial issue in their time of weakness will determine their friendship or hostility for the US a generation hence when their importance in world politics may be substantially greater. Thus failure to demonstrate an appreciation today of African aspirations may eventually (a) forfeit great influence to the communist powers, who have taken a clear position in support of black states and liberation movements and (b) jeopardize our strategic and economic interests in non-white Africa. Any anti-US or pro-communist reactions, however, are unlikely to be either solid or early, and many black states are very aware of the dangers of association with the communists.

Other Tangible Interests: Others reply that our interests in the white states of southern Africa - albeit having a relatively low priority among such interests worldwide - are clearly worth retaining at their present political cost. These interests include access to air and naval facilities for which alternatives are expensive or less satisfactory, a major space tracking station, and significant investment and balance of trade advantages. Our political concerns and other interests may be accommodated because (a) the great majority of non-white states in Africa and elsewhere will put their own immediate self-interest ahead of penalizing us for our interests in the white states, and (b) even the most directly involved black states (Zambia and Tanzania) will temper their reaction because our continued good will and support for their cause will be important, and they know it. In any event other countries will judge our standing on the racial issue worldwide by the outcome of the racial problems in the United States.

III.
PRESENT POLICY

The aim of present policy is to try to balance
our economic, scientific and strategic interests
in the white states with the political interest
of dissociating the US from the white minority
regimes and their repressive racial policies.
Decisions have been made ad hoc, on a judgment
of benefits and political costs at a given
moment. But the strength of this policy - its
flexibility - is also its weakness. Policy is
not precisely recorded. And because there have
been significant differences of view within the
government as to how much weight should be given
to these conflicting factors in any given instance, certain decisions have been held in sus-
pense "pending review of the over-all policy" -
e.g. visits of naval vessels to South African
ports enroute to and from the Indian Ocean or
Vietnam, export licensing of equipment for South
Africa, Angola and Mozambique, which might be
used either for military or civilian purposes,
participation of South African military personnel in Department of Defense correspondence
courses.

This policy seeks progress toward majority
rule through political arrangements which guarantee increasing participation by the whole
population. Tangible evidence of such progress
has been considered a precondition for improved
US relations with the white states. In the case
of South Africa, the following are illustrative
of the types of actions which that government
might take to improve relations with the US:

A. Bilateral. Permit assignment of non-whites
to US Embassy and consulates. Non-discriminatory
treatment of US naval personnel and merchant

marine crews ashore. Non-discriminatory visa
policy. Permit more South African non-whites in
US exchange programs. Facilitate US official
access to non-white areas of South Africa and
South West Africa.

B. Internal. Eliminate job reservation and
abolish pay differentials based on race. Recognize African labor unions as bargaining units.
Abolish pass laws and repressive security
legislation. Move towards qualified franchise
for non-whites.

C. Regional and International. Recognize UN
responsibility for South West Africa and permit
UN presence in territory; cease applying repressive legislation there. Withdraw economic and
paramilitary support from Rhodesia. Give gener-
ous customs treatment to Botswana, Lesotho and
Swaziland. Expand exceptions to apartheid in
cases of visiting non-whites such as sportsmen
and businessmen.

(It is realized that most of the foregoing
are unrealistic under present circumstances, but
they illustrate the directions in which change
might be sought.)

Following are the actions taken toward the
different countries and areas which, in sum,
constitute our present policy toward southern
Africa:

Republic of South Africa

We maintain limited but formally correct
diplomatic relations, making clear our opposition
to apartheid. In the early 1960s the US played
a leading role in the UN in denouncing South
Africa's racial policies. We led the effort in
1963 to establish and we continue to support the
UN arms embargo on South Africa. We have avoided
association with the South African Defense
Forces except for limited military attache contacts. We supported the UN declaration that
South Africa's mandate over South West Africa
had terminated, and calling for it to withdraw
and to acknowledge direct UN responsibility for
the territory. On the other hand, we have acted

94

on the premise that the problems of South Africa
and South West Africa do not justify either use
of force or the imposition of mandatory economic
sanctions, in part because there is no evidence
that these actions would be efficacious. Moreover, we have sought to avoid the involvement of
any US military forces which might be required
for such measures. Negro personnel have not been
assigned to the US mission and consulates in
South Africa.

We have supported efforts to protect the
legal rights of victims of discriminatory and
repressive legislation in South Africa and South
West Africa. This has involved aid memoires,
attendance at trials to assure international
observation of certain legal and judicial practices, and cooperation with private groups in
the American bar to reinforce in South Africa
traditions of respect for the rule of law. We
also have sought to deepen our identification
with the non-white majorities through personnal
contacts, public appearances and our exchange
program. We have sought to support through the
UN and private agencies humanitarian relief for
South African and South West African victims of
repression.

There is limited overflight and landing
activity by US aircraft in South Africa. Except
for three emergencies, there have been no US
naval ship calls in South African ports since
early 1967, pending a review of policy towards
South Africa. We rely heavily on the NASA tracking station near Johannesburg, particularly for
planetary missions, but at the same time maintain less satisfactory alternate facilities outside South Africa in case it becomes necessary
or desirable to close the station. The future
need for the DOD tracking station at Pretoria is
under review. The tentative conclusions are that
the station is no longer required for research
and development of missiles. We enjoy very
profitable economic relations with South Africa
despite the official approach of neither encouraging nor discouraging investment (apart from
the Foreign Direct Investment Program) and
keeping trade facilitative services in low key.
EXIM loans are not authorized, but export

guarantees up to five years are permitted, subject to review for political implications. In general, the restrictions imposed on our economic relations with South Africa, especially the constraints on EXIM financing, may have limited somewhat the growth of our exports and investment there. Profit prospects in South Africa, however, attract US business regardless of official endorsement.

Southern Rhodesia

The US voted for the Security Council resolutions of December, 1966, and May, 1968, which imposed mandatory sanctions against Southern Rhodesia on the basis of a finding of a threat to the peace under Chapter VII of the UN Charter. Executive Orders implementing the sanctions program were issued in January, 1967, and July, 1968, under authority of the UN Participation Act of 1945. (Although Portugal and South Africa have assisted Southern Rhodesia, the US has not supported the extension of mandatory sanctions to them.)

The mandatory sanctions program was devised by the British as a compromise between the use of force, which they were unwilling to contemplate largely because of domestic considerations, and doing nothing, which would have jeopardized their relations with the black African states and other Afro-Asian members of the Commonwealth. The United States cooperated with the UK largely for the same reasons. We also anticipated that failure to devise peaceful means to influence the Smith regime toward a satisfactory settlement would encourage extremists and dangerous instability in the area. Although it was recognized from the start that the sanctions program would be an imperfect instrument there was a tendency to overestimate the effectiveness of sanctions, which have been weakened by numerous and sometimes large (South Africa and Portugal) loopholes. Similarly, although there was awareness that the convenience of certain economic interests would be disrupted through sanctions, there was a tendency to under-

estimate the extent to which criticism, both
political and economic, would multiply with the
passage of time and evidence of the program's
lack of success.

The US has continued to recognize British
sovereignty in the colony, and refused to support
the use of force by either side to the dispute.
We maintain a reduced staff at our Consulate
General in Salisbury which continues to operate
under exequaturs from the British Crown. With
the Southern Rhodesian determination to declare
itself a republic, increasingly negative reactions may be anticipated from African nations
to our continuing presence in Salisbury. The
Consulate General provides citizenship and welfare services to approximately 1100 American
residents, three-fourths of whom are missionary
families.

Portuguese Territories

Our approach to Angola and Mozambique is
influenced by countervailing factors. On the one
hand Portugal is a NATO ally which we equip with
arms and whose islands, the Azores, we find important for use as an air base. On the other
hand we sympathize with the aspirations of the
Angolans and Mozambicans for self-determination.

In implementation of these policies we maintain a unilateral embargo on military equipment
for use in the Portuguese territories either
directly or through our NATO supplies to Portugal. US export controls restrain possible sales
of dual-purpose items, such as jet transports
and communications equipment to the government
of Portugal for uses in Africa.

We cooperate with Portugal on NATO matters
and continue to use the Azores facilities. US
naval vessels and aircraft also use facilities
in the Portuguese African territories for re-
fuelling and space support missions. Trade relations with the territories are normal and there
are no USG restraints on American investment
there apart from the Foreign Direct Investment
Program. EXIM Bank facilities are available,
subject to review for political implications.

Black African States of Southern Africa

The US maintains cordial relations with the
five black-ruled states of the area, Malawi,
Zambia, Botswana, Lesotho, and Swaziland. We
have Ambassadors in Malawi and Zambia. Since
their independence we have maintained Charges in
Botswana, Lesotho and Swaziland and these countries are pressing us for the assignment of
resident Ambassadors. These countries consider
the level of our diplomatic representatives to
be an important manifestation of US sympathy
and support.

As with all developing countries, an important
factor in our relations is the level and kind of
aid we can provide. Under current policies AID
provides funds for regional and multi-donor projects and for the small Special Self-Help and
Development Program. Investment guarantees are
available, and the US extends additional help
through PL 480 food donations, and Peace Corps
programs in four of the five black countries.
However, there is a body of opinion which considers that programs of bilateral technical
assistance are necessary in these states because of their generally isolated and enclave
location. Bilateral assistance has been limited
as a matter of policy to 10 concentration countries in Africa, none of which are in the southern region. World-wide AID policy is currently
under review (See Annex 7 for a discussion of
considerations involved in bilateral aid to the
black states of the region.)

A further problem with these countries is the
Conte amendment to foreign assistance legislation. Zambia, fearful of attacks by the white
regimes in retaliation for passage of liberation
groups through her territory, is purchasing air
defense missiles and possibly jet aircraft from
the UK and Italy. The Conte amendment requires
the cancellation of US aid of bilateral and some
regional types in the amount of weapons expenditures. We have introduced legislation to change
the amendment to provide greater flexibility.
Despite our explanations of the intent of Congress, application of the Conte amendment may be
seen by the black states as evidence that the

US is more sympathetic to the status quo of the white regimes than the aspirations of the blacks.

Liberation Groups

The US maintains contact with exile nationalist movements from the white-controlled states. We also assist refugee students from these states through the Southern African Student Program and two secondary schools which are operated for refugee students. The US takes the position that force is not an appropriate means to bring about constructive change in southern Africa.

United Nations

On southern African issues in the UN the relationship between the US position and that of Afro-Asian UN members has altered considerably over the last five years. We played a leading role in the arms embargo against South Africa, the determination that South Africa's mandate over South West Africa has terminated, and on mandatory economic sanctions against Southern Rhodesia. However, these actions largely exhausted the store of measures we were prepared to take on these issues.

The Afro-Asians have steadily increased pressures to exclude South Africa from the UN, for sanctions against South Africa and Portugal, and for use of force to give effect to UN actions. These demands have moved these states far out in front of the US and some other Free World countries. We have consistently resisted efforts to exclude South Africa from international bodies and to extend mandatory sanctions or use force on southern African issues. Thus the US has made it clear that we have gone as far as we can in the direction of greater UN pressures on the white regimes. (The UK and France have adopted an even more restrained position on southern African issues, in their abstentions on the UN General Assembly resolution determining that South Africa's mandate over South West Africa had terminated on which we voted in favor, and the UK's somewhat more

permissive policy on the arms embargo against
South Africa, which is virtually a dead letter
in the case of France.)

IV. THE RANGE
OF POLICY OPTIONS

US Objectives

There are several broad objectives of US policy toward southern Africa. Arranged without intent to imply priority, they are:

- To improve the US standing in black Africa and internationally on the racial issue.
- To minimize the likelihood of escalation of violence in the area and the risk of US involvement.
- To minimize the opportunities for the USSR and Communist China to exploit the racial issue in the region for propaganda advantage and to gain political influence with black governments and liberation movements.
- To encourage moderation of the current rigid racial and colonial policies of the white regimes.
- To protect economic, scientific and strategic interests and opportunities in the region, including the orderly marketing of South Africa's gold production.

These objectives are to a degree contradictory - pursuit of one may make difficult the successful pursuit of one or more of the others. Moreover, views as to the relative priority among these objectives vary widely, depending primarily upon the perception of the nature of the problems in the area and US interest there (see II(B)).

Range of Choice

The general policy question centers on US posture toward the white regimes - a key ele-

ment in our relations with the black states in
the area and a factor of varying degree of
importance throughout the continent.

But the range of feasible policy options is
limited. On one extreme our interests do not
justify considerations of US military intervention in the area. Similarly economic sanctions
against Portugal or South Africa are excluded
both because they are likely to be ineffective
and because they could lead to a US military involvement in their enforcement. On the other
extreme we cannot accept or endorse either the
racial or colonial policies of the white regimes.
Nor can we identify ourselves with violent or
repressive solutions to the area's problems on
either side of the confrontation. The essential
choice is among:

(a) closer association with the white regimes
to protect and enhance our economic, strategic
and scientific interests (Option 1),
(b) broader association with both black and
white states in an effort to encourage moderation in the white states, to enlist cooperation of the black states in reducing tensions
and the likelihood of increasing cross-border
violence, and to encourage improved relations
among states in area (Option 2),
(c) limited association with the white states
and closer association with the blacks in an
effort to retain some economic, scientific and
strategic interests in the white states while
maintaining a posture on the racial issue
which the blacks will accept, though opposing
violent solutions to the problems of the
region (Option 3),
(d) dissociation from the white regimes with
closer relations with the black states in an
effort to enhance our standing on the racial
issue in Africa and internationally (Option 4),
(e) dissociation from both black and white
states in an effort to limit our involvement
in the problems of the area (Option 5).

Each option represents a range of actions,
with some flexibility of choice among specific
means without altering the premise or general

102

strategy of the option. The purpose of this paper is to afford the NSC a choice on basic posture toward southern Africa. It is not intended to be a specific scenario for operational action, and the examples in each option are the types of action which would be consistent with the option's thrust but are neither comprehensive nor necessarily in each case the specific action which would be selected.

A satisfactory arrangement regarding South Africa's handling of gold can continue to be sought under any of the options, but it might be more difficult to achieve under Options 4 and 5.

Option 1

Premise:

We recognize the long-term dangers resulting from white regime race policies, but we can have no significant affect on the situation in the region. The whites are in control and insurgent violence will not seriously threaten that control. We cannot change the domestic policies of the white regimes - nor should our disagreement with those policies govern our relations with either the black states or white states in the region. In these circumstances our economic, scientific and strategic interests in the region, primarily in the white states, are worth preserving and expanding. The political costs of closer relations with the white states will not be excessive.

General Posture:

We would expand our contacts and economic, scientific, and strategic activities in white-dominated states and territories. We would maintain normal relations with the black states of the region to the extent they would permit, but we would assume the risks of reaction against us in the black areas of the region and the rest of Africa which such policies toward the white states might stimulate. Without formally undermining the British and UN position in Rhodesia, we would be more flexible in our attitude toward the Smith regime. We would accept South Africa's continued strong influence on Botswana, Lesotho and Swaziland. We would continue diplomatic and modest economic relations with the black states unless they took the initiative to cut them off.

Operational Examples:

- Relax arms embargo against South Africa with liberal treatment of equipment which could serve either military or civilian purposes or which could serve the common defense (e.g. ASW equipment).
- Authorize routine naval visits and use of airfields.
- Retain tracking stations in South Africa as long as required.
- Actively promote US exports to South Africa, South West Africa, and Portugues Territories; facilitate US investment in these areas within framework of US Foreign Direct Investment Program; remove constraints on EXIM Bank facilities.
- Permit unlimited dealings with South African authorities in the territory.
- Relax enforcement of sanctions against Rhodesia (e.g. hardship exceptions for chrome); retain consulate; if Republic is declared consider eventual recognition.
- Relax the unilateral US arms embargo on the Portuguese territories to permit export of dual purpose equipment.
- Limit economic aid to the black states to regional and multi-donor programs; give no arms aid; seek no change in Conte amendment.
- Publicly discourage insurgent movements.
- Maintain existing information and exchange activities in both white and black states.

PROS:

1. Preserves and offers opportunity to expand US scientific and strategic interests in the white regimes of southern Africa.
2. Expands profitable US market and investment opportunities.

3. Removes an irritant in US relations with Portugal.
4. Establishes friendly relations with the strongest powers in the region today.

CONS:

1. Policy does nothing to deal with the problems of racial repression and potential violent confrontation in the region. The whites will view it as vindication of their policies and the blacks will consider it as a betrayal of their cause.
2. Deepens our involvement with the white regimes in the face of probable growing racial violence.
3. Identification with the white regimes will damage our standing elsewhere in Africa and internationally on the racial issue. As the full impact of our policy became evident, it could be increasingly difficult to maintain access to and enjoyment of some of the strategic and economic advantages we now enjoy in Africa outside of the region.
4. Forfeits to the Communist powers influence with the black states of the region and to some extent with those elsewhere in Africa, and in the insurgent movements.
5. Unilateral US relaxation of sanctions against Rhodesia would be a highly visible violation of our international obligations and would be damaging both to the US and to the UN.

Option 2

Premise:

The whites are here to stay and the only way that constructive change can come about is through them. There is no hope for the blacks to gain the political rights they seek through violence, which will only lead to chaos and increased opportunities for the communists. We can, by selective relaxation of our stance toward the white regimes, encourage some modification of

their current racial and colonial policies and
through more substantial economic assistance to
the black states (a total of about $5 million
annually in technical assistance to the black
states) help to draw the two groups together and
exert some influence on both for peaceful change.
Our tangible interests form a basis for our contacts in the region, and these can be maintained
at an acceptable political cost.

General Posture:

We would maintain public opposition to racial
repression but relax political isolation and
economic restrictions on the white states. We
would begin by modest indications of this relaxation, broadening the scope of our relations
and contacts gradually and to some degree in
response to tangible - albeit small and gradual
- moderation of white policies. Without openly
taking a position undermining the UK and the UN
on Rhodesia, we would be more flexible in our
attitude toward the Smith regime. We would take
present Portuguese policies as suggesting further
changes in the Portuguese territories. At the
same time we would take diplomatic steps to convince the black states of the area that their
current liberation and majority rule aspirations
in the south are not attainable by violence and
that their only hope for a peaceful and prosperous future lies in closer relations with
white-dominated states. We would emphasize our
belief that closer relations will help to bring
change in the white states. We would give increased and more flexible economic aid to black
states of the area to focus their attention on
their internal development and to give them a
motive to cooperate in reducing tensions. We
would encourage economic assistance from South
Africa to the developing black nations.

This option accepts, at least over a 3 to 5
year period, the prospect of unrequited US
initiatives toward the whites and some opposition
from the blacks in order to develop an atmosphere
conducive to change in white attitudes through
persuasion and erosion. To encourage this change
in white attitudes, we would indicate our will-

106

ingness to accept political arrangements short
of guaranteed progress toward majority rule, provided that they assure broadened political participation in some form by the whole population.

The various elements of the option would stand
as a whole and approval of the option would not
constitute approval of individual elements out
of this context.

Operational Examples:

- Enforce arms embargo against South Africa
  but with liberal treatment of equipment
  which could serve either military or civilian purposes.
- Permit US naval calls in South Africa with
  arrangements for non-discrimination toward
  US personnel in organized activity ashore;
  authorize routine use of airfields.
- Retain tracking stations in South Africa as
  long as required.
- Remove constraints on EXIM Bank facilities
  for South Africa; actively encourage US exports and facilitate US investment consistent
  with the Foreign Direct Investment Program.
- Conduct selected exchange programs with
  South Africa in all categories, including
  military.
- Without changing the US legal position that
  South African occupancy of South West Africa
  is illegal, we would play down the issue and
  encourage accommodation between South Africa
  and the UN.
- On Rhodesia, retain consulate; gradually
  relax sanctions (e.g. hardship exceptions for
  chrome) and consider eventual recognition.
- Continue arms embargo on Portuguese territories, but give more liberal treatment to
  exports of dual purpose equipment.
- Encourage trade and investment in Portuguese
  territories; full EXIM Bank facilities.
- Establish flexible aid programs in the black
  states of the region; respond to reasonable
  requests for purchase of non-sophisticated
  arms but seek no change in Conte amendment.
- Toward African insurgent movements take
  public position that US opposes use of force

in racial confrontation. Continue humanitarian assistance to refugees.
- Increase information and exchange activities
in both white and black states.

PROS:

1. Encourages existing tendencies to broaden
relations between black states and white and
thus reduce tensions - South Africa's new outward policy, Zambia's trade and sub rosa political contacts with South Africa and Portugal.
2. Preserves US economic, scientific and strategic interests in the white states and would
expand opportunities for profitable trade and
investment.
3. Relaxation of the US attitude toward the
whites could help lift their present siege
mentality; and it would encourage elements
among the whites seeking to extend South
African relationships with black Africa.
4. US diplomatic support and economic aid
offer the black states an alternative to the
recognized risks of mounting communist
influence.
5. Increased aid would also give us greater
influence to caution the black states against
violent confrontation and give them a tangible
stake in accepting the prospects of gradual
change.
6. Would reduce a major irritant in our relations with Portugal, and afford the Caetano
government opportunity for liberalization.

CONS:

1. Relaxation of US stance towards white
states could be taken by the whites as a
vindication of their policies. Many black
states, led by Zambia and Tanzania, probably
would charge us with subordinating our professed ideals to material interests and
tolerating white-regime policies.
2. There is a serious question whether pro-
Western leaders of the black states could
continue to justify their stance to their
populations if the US officially declared its

opposition to current liberation efforts.
Radical and communist states would be the
beneficiaries.
3. Unilateral US relaxation of sanctions
against Rhodesia would be a highly visible
violation of our international obligations
and would be damaging both to the US and to
the UN.
4. The current thrust of South African
domestic policy does not involve any basic
change in the racial segregation system,
which is anathema to the black states. There
is virtually no evidence that changes might
be forthcoming in these South African policies
as a result of any approach on our part.
5. Requires extensive diplomatic and economic
involvement in a situation in which the solution is extremely long-range and the outcome
doubtful at best.
6. It is doubtful that the additional aid
contemplated would be sufficiently great to
influence the black states in the direction
indicated.

Option 3

Premise:

The situation in the region is not likely to
change appreciably in the foreseeable future, and
in any event we cannot influence it. Consequently
we can retain some economic, scientific and stragetic interests in the white states at the same
time as we protect our world-wide standing on the
racial issue by limiting the nature and scope of
our associations with these states and by increasing our aid to the black states of the
region. To do so provides us with a posture of
flexibility to enable us best to adapt our
policy to future trends.

General Posture:

This is a codification and extension of present policy.
In the UN and bilaterally we could continue
basic opposition to the racial and colonial poli-

cies of the white states but seek to maintain
correct relations with them. We would retain some
military access, scientific installations etc.,
under conditions which do not imply our condoning
of racial repression. In concert with the British,
we would stand firmly against the Smith regime,
closing our consulate and continuing sanctions.
We would ease pressures on Portugal to encourage
liberalizing tendencies of the Caetano government towards Africa. We would give economic aid
to black states of the region. We would continue
to oppose violent solutions to the problems of
the region, and to oppose the outward thrust of
South African influence where this strengthens
South African domination of neighboring states.

Operational Examples:

- Strict application of arms embargo against
  South Africa.
- Permit US naval calls in South Africa with
  arrangements for non-discrimination toward
  US personnel ashore.
- Retain NASA station in South Africa but with
  alternative facilities elsewhere.
- Neither encourage nor discourage investment
  in South Africa, give low-key commercial
  services, no direct EXIM Bank loans but permit insurance and guarantees of commercial
  credits.
- Continue to view South African administration
  of South West Africa as illegal; urge South
  Africa to accept UN supervisory authority;
  discourage US investment; no EXIM facilities.
- Follow British lead on representation and
  recognition of Southern Rhodesia and on UN
  sanctions program; withdraw consulate.
- Maintain arms embargo on Portuguese territories, take neutral attitude on investment
  and permit EXIM facilities for US exports
  short of major infrastructural projects.
  Soften criticisms of Portuguese African
  policy in UN and bilaterally.
- Establish flexible economic assistance programs in the black states of the region;
  seek legislation to soften Conte restrictions.
- Maintain discreet contact with African in-

surgent movements and extend educational and
humanitarian assistance to individuals.
- Maintain modest information and exchange
  programs in white-ruled areas (except Rhodesia); expand activities in the black states.

PROS:

1. Preserves most of our major economic,
scientific and strategic interests in region
at least in the short run.
2. Affords access to black states in the
region and preserves some standing elsewhere
in Africa and with Afro-Asian states at the
UN.
3. Retains some flexibility for movement
closer to either white or black states, depending upon future developments.
4. Would result in some improvement in our
relations with Portugal.

CONS:

1. Position would be seen as expedient and
hypocritical by both sides. Our condemnation
of whites hurts us with them, yet fails to
satisfy the blacks, exposing us to pressures
for more decisive measures.
2. Policy does nothing to deal actively with
problem of violence in the area of increasing
communist influence.
3. Restrictions on association with white
regimes involve some loss of potential US
economic and defense assets.
4. Even limited association with white regimes is vulnerable to exploitation by the
communists and African extremists.
5. Closer relations with Portugal could
adversely affect our relations with Zambia
and Tanzania.

Option 4

Premise:

We cannot influence the white states for
constructive change, and therefore increasing
violence is likely.

Only by cutting our ties with the white regimes can we protect our standing on the race issue in black Africa and internationally. Since our tangible interest are not vital, this is a reasonable price to pay.

General Posture:

We would maintain minimal relations with the white regimes, emphasizing that improved relations are impossible until they moderate present policies. Make clear to black states the extent to which the US has cut dealings with white regimes. We would take no actions in the white states which would run the least risk of political repercussions in the black states. We would take positive official stands against racial and colonial repression. We would afford economic aid to black states of region and sell reasonable quantities of non-sophisticated defensive military equipment. We would stress our support for black objectives short of force or sanctions against South Africa and Portugal. For maximum effectiveness of this option, an effort would be made to enlist international support behind the policy.

Operational Examples:

- Reduce diplomatic mission and consulates in South Africa.
- Strictest application of arms embargo against South Africa.
- Remove military and NASA tracking stations.
- Prohibit official use of South African ports and airfields except in emergency.
- Discourage investment, no commercial services or EXIM facilities in South Africa.
- Make clear that we regard South Africa's continued occupation of South West Africa as illegal. Discourage US investment; deny commercial services and EXIM facilities; hold to minimum US contacts with South African authorities in South West Africa.
- Support expansion and stricter international enforcement of sanctions and maintain non-

recognition of Southern Rhodesia; withdraw consulate.

- Limit EXIM Bank activities and official trade promotion in Portuguese territories. Maintain arms embargo and political pressures on Portuguese.
- Establish flexible economic assistance programs in the black states of the region; seek legislation to soften Conte restrictions; respond sympathetically to requests for nonsophisticated defensive arms by Zambia.
- Open contact and sympathy for aspirations of African insurgent groups short of material support.
- Reduce information and exchange programs in white areas to a minimum; expand programs in the black states.

PROS:

1. Would significantly increase our credibility in black Africa and the UN by demonstrating US is prepared to back its pronouncements on the race issue at some material sacrifices.
2. Provides maximum leverage to limit Soviet and Chinese influence among liberation groups and in their host countries.
3. Would put white regimes on notice that US is not prepared to bail them out for material or strategic reasons.
4. Would provide opportunity for US to join multilateral effort to achieve change in white-regime racial policies.

CONS:

1. It would increase our involvement with the insurgent movements, would tend to identify us with their cause, and would stimulate demands for more far-reaching action.
2. Sacrifices economic, strategic and scientific interests.
3. France, the UK and other major trading nations are unlikely to support us. This will weaken effectiveness of pressures and forfeit economic opportunities to others.

4. Will probably reinforce the siege mentality of the white regimes. There is no evidence that the white regimes of southern Africa will make constructive changes in their race policies in response to external pressure.
5. Would make our relations with the Portuguese more difficult.

Option 5

Premise:

The racial confrontation in southern Africa is unmanageable and potentially dangerous and will grow worse despite any efforts we might make. Thus we should lower our profile in the area and avoid identification with either side.

General Posture:

We would maintain correct but minimal relations with both black and white states in the area. We would cut or sharply reduce ties with the white states, making clear to them that we regard their policies as disastrous and cannot be associated with them. We would take the position, however, that the nature and extent of measures they take to resolve their racial problems are matters for them to decide and are of no direct concern to us. We would make clear to the black states that while we sympathize with their objectives and oppose the racial and colonial policies of the white regimes, we cannot support them in an un-realistic struggle or become involved in a racial conflict. Violence is not in their long-run interest and can only heighten the dangers of communist involvement. We would take positive official stands both against racial and colonial repression and against insurgent violence but we would resist efforts in the UN for stronger measures to deal with southern African issues.

Operational Examples:

- Reduce size of our diplomatic and consular offices to the minimum.
- Withdraw consultate from Rhodesia, continue

114

sanctions (with one-time hardship exception for chrome); refuse recognition.
- Remove NASA and defense tracking stations.
- Prohibit official use of ports or airfields in the white states except in emergencies.
- Strictest enforcement of arms embargoes.
- No official encourgement of investment and no EXIM facilities or commerical services to facilitate trade with the white states.
- Limit aid to black states to regional or multi-donor programs. No arms aid. Seek no change in Conte amendment.
- Public discouragement of insurgent movements.
- Continue to resist stronger measures in the UN and mute statements on Southern African issues.
- Reduce to a minimum all information and exchange programs with the region.

PROS:

1. Relieves pressure in the UN and elsewhere which flowed from our diplomatic "leadership" in an area not of vital concern to us.
2. By removing the inherent equivocation – tangible interests versus political credibility – in present policy, this option gives us maximum flexibility to cope with pressures for greater involvement which will continue in this problem whatever our policy.
3. To the degree that we disengage from the white states and disavow our intervention in an African problem, we strengthen our political position in the developing world.
4. Since we would make clear that neither side can count on our support in a major confrontation, our posture could lessen the danger of miscalculations which both whites and blacks may now harbor.

CONS:

1. Sacrifices US economic, scientific and strategic interests in the area, particularly those in the white states.
2. Foregoes influence on both sides and does nothing to ease racial confrontation.

3. Disengagement will not ultimately satisfy the blacks, and our withdrawal of support will be at the expense of rising Communist influence in the black states and liberation movements.
4. Muting support in the UN for majority rule could diminish support for us on East–West issues.
5. As a world power, we cannot disengage from an area in which the Soviets and Chinese communists have shown interest and to which our citizens and capital are attracted by opportunities.

V. THE AREA:
SITUATION, PROSPECTS
AND US INTEREST

The Situation. Southern Africa designates the area composed of Zambia, Malawi, Southern Rhodesia, Mozambique, Angola, South West Africa, South Africa, Swaziland, Lesotho, and Botswana. Some four million whites in South Africa, Namibia (South West Africa), Southern Rhodesia, Angola and Mozambique dominate 30 million blacks. (See Annex 1 for population breakdown by country). The whites, extremely conscious of world criticism, desire friendly relations with the West but not at the price of possible loss of political control. The white governments are tough, determined, and increasingly self-confident. They are also technically advanced, and their efficient security apparatuses pervade the region. They are stepping up their security cooperation with one another. South African expenditures for defense have increased seven hundred percent in the last eight years, and recent legislation creating a Bureau of State Security to coordinate all South African security functions can play an important part in improving the security cooperation among the white regimes.

African nationalist movements, supported by the Organisation of African Unity (OAU - including all African states except the white regimes), and by communist countries and organizations, are trying to overthrow the white minority regimes. (See Annex 5 for detailed description of liberation groups.) OAU support has not been large. Contributions to the OAU African Liberation Committee by African states dwindled from around two million dollars in recent years to less then one million in 1968. So far, armed African activity has been significant only in parts of the Portuguese colonies of Angola and Mozambique and, to a much less extent, in Southern Rhodesia. In

117

Portuguese Africa, outside help and sanctuary for guerrillas have helped sustain chronic guerrilla warfare. There have been sporadic incursions of guerrilla bands into Southern Rhodesia. South Africa has not experienced any guerrilla activity, although there have been incidents of urban terrorism and there was a short-lived incursion into northern South West Africa in 1966.

Grouped geographically and economically with this relatively powerful complex of white-ruled states are the black-ruled countries of southern Africa - Zambia, Malawi, Botswana, Lesotho, and Swaziland. They are, in varying degrees economically dependent on the white states. Committed to a non-racial philosophy, all of them are torn between their vulnerability to pressures by the white regimes, and sympathy for their fellow blacks. The black states have varying economic prospects. Lesotho and Swaziland are ministates, the former poor, the latter with modest resources. Botswana is large in area but sparsely populated; recent mineral discoveries have improved its economic prospects. Malawi is squeezed between spiraling population growth and scanty resources. Zambia has ample resources but has achieved real development only in enclaves dominated by foreign capital and managerial skills. All black-ruled countries in the area need outside aid if they are to develop, or in some cases, just to stay even.

Outside the region the southern African problem presents at least partly conflicting issues of US relationships on each side of the black-white line. The United Nations, with the African states making up about one-third of the membership, is one important forum in which these relationships determine attitudes towards the US. Reactions of hostility or friendship toward the US by the white regimes of southern Africa and by black African states may come to affect our access to the respective areas. Thus, hostility or friendship may affect our $2.5 billion investment in Africa, one-third in the white regime areas, two-thirds in the rest of the continent, or our foreign trade with Africa, forty percent in the white-controlled areas, sixty percent in the remainder (see Annex 9 for figures on US exports and direct investment). The sector of US economic activities outside southern Africa shows a growing favorable US balance of payments significance: in the case of Libya it is estimated at $250 to $300 million per year net inflow.

The White-ruled States

South Africa is the hard core of southern Africa. Racism is stark, harsh, and strongly entrenched. It is the most highly developed state in Africa. Security forces are strong and effective.

Status. Over the past 20 years, South Africa's racial policies have steadily hardened. Apartheid - racial separation - is the dominant ideology and the way of life. The government insists on the need to force the physical separation of whites and non-whites. The policy of "separate development" theoretically offers blacks a chance to advance in their own separate territorial "homelands" or "Bantustans", but in practice the whites do not conceal their determination to stay on top and use the Bantustans as labor pools from which migrants travel to white areas to fulfill temporary labor contracts. The regime's racial policies have been to some extent at cross purposes with the needs of the economy: at the same time that separation of races has been pushed, the booming economy has demanded an even greater supply of black labor. At the same time as the African participation in the economy has increased, the level of repression to enforce apartheid has been stepped up.

The government has not thus far been willing to make the investment that the Bantustans require; moreover they cover only 13 percent of South Africa's land area, while the black population accounts for 68 percent of the total population. (The unequal distribution of land would not be critical if South Africa were willing to make a major investment in the Bantustans to make them economically productive.) Party politics and linguistic divisions notwithstanding, South Africa's European community is increasingly united on the issue of white supremacy and fears change as a threat not only to its economic and political position, but also to its physical security. The growth of this unity is ascribed as a reaction to the acts of sabotage within South Africa 1960-65, to the increasingly militant stance of the blacks elsewhere in Africa, and to UN and other international pressures.

Inside South Africa there have been few manifestations of resistance by the black population in the last three or four years. Such information as we do have emerges in trials conducted under the Terrorism or Suppression of Communism Acts. Any non-white engaging in independent political activity is banned or imprisoned, so resistance efforts are continually drained of leadership. However, there has been some student political activity in the African universities.

Internationally, the movement to isolate South Africa has been developing since about 1960. The Afro-Asian states continue to press on world opinion in an effort to force changes on the South West African and apartheid issues or, failing that, to ostracize South Africa. The USSR and Communist China, with no material interests to lose in southern Africa and hopeful of gain in the rest of the continent, give strong verbal support to this thrust but have thus far been leary of commitments. The Western Democracies, caught between material interests and a political commitment to human equality, have had varying approaches. The US played a key role in bringing about the UN arms embargo (see Annex 10 for the text of Ambassador Stevenson's Aug. 2, 1963 speech in the UN Security Council) and has supported successive UN resolutions which have emphasized South Africa's isolation while stopping short of economic sanctions. France, which abstained on the basic August 1963 UN Security Council arms embargo resolution, has maintained an interpretation of the embargo under which it can supply strategic - as opposed to directly suppressive - equipment. With this interpretation they have supplied a range of equipment including submarines, airplanes, helicopters and armoured cars. South Africa's main international objective is to retain its ties with the West, by emphasizing its economic importance (as a seller, a

market and a major source of gold) and its stragetic potential (defense of the Cape route).

Prime Minister Vorster has launched an "outward policy" seeking to develop the external
relations of South Africa first in the region,
and later in the whole continent. The aim of
this policy is largely through economic incen-
tives to induce African countries to enter some
degree of cooperation with South Africa, thus
breaking South Africa's isolation and eventually
reducing liberation pressures. Under this policy,
racial confrontation would be replaced by peaceful coexistence between the black states, eventually including the Bantustans, and the white-ruled
states. The only African state thus far to exchange diplomatic representation under this
policy is Malawi, but there have been extensive
contacts with Botswana, Lesotho and Swaziland,
the Malagasy Republic, and even Gabon and the
Ivory Coast.

Prospects: Political freedom has been progressively curtailed over recent decades. The
white minority has a monopoly of force which it
does not hesitate to use, and of power which it
will not voluntarily yield. While the political
activity permitted the blacks in the Transkei
(largest of the projected African self-governing
areas) has given them some voice in the direction
of their affairs, the retention of basic powers
by the central government has seriously circum-
scribed its significance. Prosperity has benefited Africans as well as whites, but has had no
significant affect upon the political or social
system. The economic boom has undercut the
Bantustan program of separate development by
attracting black labor to the urban areas. The
outward policy may moderate South Africa's insular outlook, but it is likely to have only
limited success under present circumstances. For
the foreseeable future South Africa will be able
to maintain internal stability and effectively
counter insurgent activity.

US Material Interests: The US has a significant economic stake in South Africa: investment
of about $700 million, (nearly 30 percent of our

121

investment in all Africa) and a substantial
favorable trade balance (over $450 million in US
exports and $250 million in US imports in 1968).
The US provides roughly 17 percent of South
Africa's imports. South Africa produces about
60 percent of the Free World's gold, and the
orderly marketing of this production is of key
importance for the maintenance of the two-tier
gold pricing system.

South Africa is the third largest Free World
supplier of uranium. When the US-South African
Atomic Energy Agreement was extended for 10
years in 1967, the South African Government informed the US that it would do nothing in its
uranium transactions to increase nuclear pro-
liferation. South Africa has played a constructive role as a permanent member of the Board of
Governors of the International Atomic Energy
Agency.

The US has a NASA satellite tracking station
and an Air Force missile tracking station in South
Africa. The future need for the Air Force station
is under review. Tentative conclusions are that
the station is no longer required for research
and development of missiles. The NASA station is
a major space tracking facility oriented towards
providing ground support to all unmanned space-
crafts and of particular importance for future
planetary missions. Because of the unique location of South Africa in relation to launchings
from Cape Kennedy, the NASA station continues to
be of primary importance to the space program.
Although alternate facilities have been constructed for use if necessary, they do not afford
equivalent support (see Annex 8). US aircraft use
South African fields for space support and other
missions. Because of the uncertainty of overflight rights in northern and central Africa,
there is US military interest in alternative
routes through southern Africa to support contingency operations in the Indian Ocean and
Middle East areas. Until 1967 the US Navy had
used South African ports for operational calls.
The issue of segregated facilities ashore arose
during the visit of the carrier FDR in 1967. Since
then, calls have been limited to three emergencies,
but the ports are available to us. Because of this

limitation, the US has made increased use of
Angolan and Mozambican ports as substitutes but
these ports cannot accommodate aircraft carriers.
The Cape route is strategically important to the
US and its Allies especially in the face of increased Soviet activity in the Indian Ocean.
South African port facilities are of long-term
stragetic importance to the conduct of operations
in the South Atlantic and Indian Oceans. With the
closing of the Suez Canal, the strategic significance of South African refueling and repair
facilities for naval operations has increased.
South African port facilities are the best in
Africa, and their availability to the Navy would
be useful in peacetime and essential in time of
war. The British Navy continues to use these
facilities.

South Africa is eager to be included in Western defense arrangements - as a sign that it is
accepted as part of the Western community. South
Africa hopes to use the small but persistent
Soviet naval presence in the Indian Ocean, as a
basis for some sort of collaboration with the US
in monitoring or surveillance, with resultant increased US naval presence in the area and use of
South African ports.

South West Africa

No solution in sight. Despite repeated United
Nations demands that South Africa cease its illegal occupation and withdraw, South Africa is
entrenching its rule and has extended its application of apartheid and repressive measures.
South Africa considers the area vital to its
security and an economic asset.

Status: Mandated to South Africa by the League
of Nations in 1920, South West Africa is the only
Mandate that did not become independent or a
United Nations Trust Territory following World
War II. Disregarding opinions of the International
Court of Justice of 1950, 1955 and 1956, South
Africa rejected UN supervision of the Mandate.
The International Court of Justice, in a close
vote in 1966, sidestepped the substantive issue
of South African administration of South West

Africa by refusing to rule on the issue on a
legal technicality. That judgment was a major
setback to hopes that a legal settlement might
be reached. Subsequently in the same year the UN
General Assembly with the UK and France abstain-
ing voted that South Africa had forfeited the
right to administer the territory and that the
United Nations assumed direct responsibility for
it. Since then, South Africa has rejected United
Nations demands for its withdrawal and has taken
steps towards annexation of the territory. Attempts toward infiltration and organized resistance in the north were crushed in 1966-67.
South West Africa is sparsely populated but has
agricultural and fisheries resources and important mineral deposits. Because of its international community, and continued South Africa
control of the territory is a source of friction
between South Africa and the rest of the world.
The UN General Assembly has established (without
support from the US or other principal Western
powers) a special Council for South West Africa
to take over administration of that territory.
Efforts by the Council to exercise such authority
have been thwarted by South Africa. The Afro-
Asian nations are increasing their pressure for
direct Security Council action, including mandatory sanctions, to establish the authority of the
special council for South West Africa.

Prospects: South Africa will continue to
occupy and administer the territory while the
African and Asian nations press for stronger
measures to force South Africa out. The South
African police and military forces will be able
to successfully counter any insurgent or dissident activity for the foreseeable future.

United States Material Interests: Major investment (valued at over $40 million) in the profit-
able Tsumeb mines (copper, lead, zinc). US firms
also prospecting for oil and minerals.

Southern Rhodesia

The complete break with the UK and the en-
trenchment of constitutional provisions for white

domination all but rule out the possibility of finding any ground for a settlement.

Status: In November, 1965, Rhodesia's white minority regime unilaterally declared its independence (UDI) from the UK. The UN Security Council, finding that the resultant situation in the region constituted a threat to international peace and security, has imposed comprehensive mandatory economic sanctions (see Annexes 3 and 4 for a discussion of sanctions and the chrome problem). The UK was willing to give independence to Smith before majority rule, but it insisted on guarantees of unimpeded movement toward majority rule. The white Rhodesians refused to accept an effective safeguard mechanism and instead in a referendum July 20, 1969, approved republic status which will end all ties with Great Britain as well as constitutional proposals which lay the groundwork for perpetuation of white control.

The white minority - 4 percent of the population of Southern Rhodesia - made the decision; no more than a handful of the blacks voted. The minority of the 4.8 million blacks in Southern Rhodesia who are politically active have been expressing their opposition to the consolidation of white rule in two ways. A small segment have directly supported the liberation groups (the Zimbabwe African Nation Union - ZANU and the Zimbabwe African Peoples Union - ZAPU), whose original leaders have been imprisioned by the white Southern Rhodesian regime. Another small group has campaigned internally to get as many Africans as possible on the voter rolls. ZANU and ZAPU have boycotted this effort and refused participation in national politics since 1961 as a protest on the grounds that the whites had no intention of moving towards majority rule.

The new constitution ensures that majority rule will not be achieved at any time, by placing whites on one voters' roll and blacks on another. Theoretical representational parity in parliament would be given to the nation's 4.8 million blacks but increased representation is based on a formula which, for all practical purposes, assures that such a balance cannot be reached. The constitutional proposals would extend censorship and preventive detention laws and enshrine in the constitution the government's right to restrict political opponents without trial or bail.

As a consequence of the referendum outcome, the British-appointed governor of Southern Rhodesia has resigned, and the British completely withdrew their residual mission in Salisbury on July 14 and the Rhodesian mission in London was closed at the same time. There is a US residual consulate accredited to the UK. West Germany, Switzerland, Italy, France, Portugal, Netherlands and South Africa also maintain consulates; Belgium has just withdrawn its office.

UN economic sanctions have constricted Rhodesia's economy and have produced a slowdown in economic development, but the whites have suffered little discomfort and there is still flexibility in the economy (see Annex 3). The curtailment of foreign investment and the reduction of economic activity have made even more difficult the absorption of the large number of Africans entering the labor force each year. South Africa has provided considerable financial assistance and limited paramilitary aid.

Portugal and South Africa have refused to enforce sanctions, and there have been reports of increasing violations of the sanctions program by certain other countries, including France, Japan and Poland.

Internationally, Rhodesia is a pariah. No state has recognized it - not even South Africa or Portugal. The South Africans and Portuguese have some reservations about an independent Southern Rhodesia as an irritant on the southern African scene stimulating insurgent activity and international pressures, but they do not want to see international sanctions work - the precedents and consequences are too dangerous.

Prospects: Despite the effects of sanctions, the white regime can hold out indefinitely with South African help. The internal security system can meet foreseeable threats. There is little chance of acceptance by the international community. Ominous signs for the future are the rapid growth of African population and lack of economic opportunities for Africans. Prospects

for meaningful negotiations with the UK have
diminished since the referendum.

US Material Interests: Rhodesia provided between a fourth and a third of US metallurgical
chromite imports before sanctions cut off this
source of supply. US-owned mines are under
Rhodesian government control. Even before UDI,
US trade including chromite was small, totaling
$33 million (exports plus imports) in 1965; US
investment is small, amounting to about $56
million.

US relations with the UK could be effected
by the degree to which we depart from their
policy position on Rhodesia.

Portuguese Territories (Angola and Mozambique)

The whites dominate the political and economic
spheres. The government is repressive but probably
not more so than in Portugal itself. However, unlike other white regimes, racial discrimination
is not legally sanctioned in the Portuguese
territories.

Status: The Portuguese have been in Angola
and Mozambique for 500 years, and consider the
territories legally part of Portugal. Multi-
racialism is official policy and racial attitudes are markedly different from those in South
Africa or Rhodesia. The Portuguese insist that
there is no color bar, only a civilization bar -
but until recently have lagged in providing educational facilities for Africans. Many of the
white settlers in both territories show racist
attitudes, although the Portuguese administration
has tried to combat this. Possibilities for political expression are very limited and confined
mostly to the European minority.
Portugal has been the object of strong condemnation in the United Nations for her colonial
policies. But some Africans seem to take a less
hostile view of Portugal than of South Africa or
Rhodesia. The Portuguese have discreet relations
and contacts with a number of African governments,
including Zambia. Liberation movements have been

waging a guerrilla war in Angola since 1961 and
in Mozambique since 1964. Portuguese fortunes have
ebbed and flowed, though lately their position
has improved somewhat in both territories.

Prospects: The outlook for the rebellions is
one of continued stalemate: the rebels cannot
oust the Portuguese and the Portuguese can contain but not eliminate the rebels. Substantial
change is only likely to come from decisions made
in Portugal although economic expansion may stimulate African pressures for change in the colonies.
There is some sign of separatist tendencies among
Angolan and Mozambican whites. Unless accompanied
by guarantees of increased participation by the
Africans, greater autonomy might put white
settlers in control and could be a backward step
in race relations. The immediate question is
whether the Caetano government will try to liber-
alize colonial policy - and how far it will be
able to go.

There are no indications that the Caetano
government has any plans for the evolution of its
African territories toward self-determination.
Caetano has made it clear that as of now plans
for liberalization are limited to achieving some
degree of administrative autonomy in territories
which are to remain part of Portugal. Behind
this position taken by the Portuguese government
lies the reality of an important and growing economic stake in the territories, particularly in
Angola. Portugal accounts for 70 percent of investment in the territories, chiefly in the
coffee, cotton, sugar, diamond mining and petroleum industries. In 1967 Portuguese trade with
the territories was valued at $314 million, or
about 18 percent of total Portuguese trade. At
their present level, economic costs and the casualties of the effort to contain the insurgency
have not undermined the will to make the continued military effort to protect these interests.

US Economic Interests and Government Activities:
The biggest US economic interest is in Angola: Gulf
Oil Company has made the Cabinda enclave (north of
the Congo River) a substantial oil producer ($125
million invested so far). US companies are pros-

pecting in Mozambique with no significant results yet. The US military make some use of Angolan and Mozambican ports and airfields, but facilities are limited (the ports cannot accommodate aircraft carriers). US exports to the two territories totalled $52 million in 1968.

US Relations with Portugal. Within the European and NATO context, there are no vital bilateral contentious issues between the US and Portugal. Our attitude towards Portugal's policies in Africa is the single major source of friction. With the forthcoming negotiations on the use of base facilities in the Azores, this fact may come into sharp focus, with the Portuguese insisting on a "more understanding" treatment by the US and a relaxation of our arms export controls.

Zambia

The most important independent black state in southern Africa.

Status: Independent since 1964, landlocked Zambia occupies a vulnerable, and in the view of the white governments, strategic position on the frontier between black and white Africa. The country's vulnerability to Rhodesian, South African and Portuguese pressures is the result of economic dependence on the white-ruled states and Zambia's relative military weakness. The main thrust of Zambian policy since Southern Rhodesia's unilateral declaration of independence has been to "disengage" from the white states by establishing alternative transport routes and facilities. The main example is the proposed TanZam railway project, from the Zambian copperbelt to the port of Dar es Salaam, Tanzania, which Chinese Communist technicians are now surveying. President Kaunda is deeply committed to the black cause in southern Africa, but has been careful to try to keep his problems with the white states manageable.

Zambian trade with the white regimes continues to be important, imports from South Africa having largely made up for the declines in trade with

Southern Rhodesia since UDI (although Zambia has very recently taken measures to cut back on South African imports). In addition, the Zambian government has had a number of sub rosa contacts with the Portuguese, both as regards Portuguese border raids and on the maintenance of copper exports on the Benguela Railroad which traverses Angola.

Since 1967, the Zambians have feared Rhodesian-South African military retaliation as a consequence of Zambia's sympathy for and limited support of the liberation movements. Portuguese military forces have occasionally crossed into Zambia and bombed Zambian villages suspected of harboring guerrillas. These attacks have not been retaliation against Zambia, but the latter has been seeking defensive military equipment - including ground-to-air missiles - to meet what it perceives to be a threat to its security.

Kaunda is a genuine multiracialist, who increasingly believes that the US is unwilling to press for majority rule and, through acquiescence, supports white regimes. He allows guerrillas to operate from Zambia against Rhodesia and Portuguese territories, but tries to keep the level of activity low enough to avoid armed retaliation or rupture of still vital economic relations. His position is sensitive, since he lacks a tribal base and his leadership is under pressure from a strong, radical tribal group led by Vice President Kapwepwe.

Prospects: Zambia shows latent instability, for tribal reasons, and may face internal crises. So far there is no one in sight who could replace Kaunda as a national leader respected by all tribal groups. Zambia will continue to seek Western help to improve its defenses, and will threaten to turn to Communist sources for arms. Zambia probably will continue to allow insurgents to pass through to Southern Rhodesia and the Portuguese territories, without officially permitting them to maintain training camps in Zambia.

US Economic Interests and Government Activities: The total US investment in Zambia of $100 million includes $75 million in Zambian copper. The US

investment represents 38 percent of the investment in the copperbelt where over 25 percent of
the world's known reserves are located. Kaunda
recently announced a shift in arrangements for
taxation of copper companies, establishment of
25-year limits on concession agreements, and the
intention of the Zambian Government to acquire a
51 percent ownership of copper companies. The US
provided oil lift when supplies were cut off
after Rhodesian UDI, and is helping to build a
highway in neighboring Tanzania that will provide
Zambia with an alternate route to the sea. Bilateral aid programs in Zambia have been small
in recent years (totalling about $4 million in
the period 1965-68) and are being phased out.
Moreover Zambia's participation in regional aid
programs has been curtailed through Conte amendment restrictions because of Zambian purchases
of sophisticated weapons. (See Annex 7 for
funding data.)

Malawi

Although opposed to segregation, President
Banda considers South African ties to be the only
realistic policy.

Status: Independent since 1964, Malawi is
caught in a squeeze between rising population and
few resources. The country's biggest export is
able-bodied males to neighboring countries. It
is ruled by the eccentric, strong-willed, Dr.
Hastings K. Banda, who won independence and now
has an iron grip on the country. Banda is strongly
pro-Western, violently anti-communist. He is also
a loner - upbraids other African countries for
their hostility to white-ruled states, has openly
established warm relations with Portugal and South
Africa. In the absence of significant aid from
other sources (except declining assistance from
the UK), the Malawian leader has decided that
South Africans and Portuguese are his best bets.
He has sought to explain his position to other
African leaders, and has had some success in
Kenya and the Malagasy Republic. The movement
into key positions in Malawi of whites with
South African racial attitudes, as a result of

131

Banda's friendly policy, has heightened racial tensions.

Prospects: The elderly Banda runs a one-man show and when he leaves the scene, Malawi may become embroiled in a factional battle over the succession. A possible outcome is a military regime, perhaps with continuing South African influence. Banda will probably continue to discourage insurgent operations into Mozambique.

US Economic Interests and Government Activities: No significant trade or investment. Bilateral aid is being phased out. US assistance, principally regional, has totalled $13.5 million since 1964 (see Annex 7 for funding data). Multi-donor and regional assistance will continue. There is also a small Peace Corps program principally in education.

Botswana, Lesotho and Swaziland

Heavily dependent on South Africa.

Status: Former British dependencies, Botswana (formerly Bechuanaland) and Lesotho (formerly Basutoland) became independent in 1966. Swaziland (no name change) became independent in 1968. All three are enclaves in white-ruled territory. Economically, they are heavily influenced by South Africa: politically, they want to develop true independence and non-racial societies, but must avoid antagonizing South Africa. Their economic assets are limited. Lesotho is the poorest, Swaziland has iron ore, asbestos, sugar, and timber resources and is closest to economic viability of the three; Botswana has proven but as yet undeveloped copper, nickel and diamond deposits.

Prospects: There is little hope Lesotho can escape the South African orbit. With greater prospects for economic progress, Botswana and, to a lesser extent Swaziland, might be able to loosen their ties with South Africa.

US Economic Interests and Government Activities: Our interests in Lesotho and Swaziland are very

small - with regard to both trade and investment.
A US-owned firm is developing the copper-nickel
deposits in Botswana. The US benefits from a UK-
operated, US-financed atmospheric nuclear test
detection station in Swaziland. The US assists
those states through the Peace Corps, PL 480, and
regional and multi-donor projects.

The US and the African States in the United Nations

The arena where the problem is most visible.

Status: In the UN African states have maintained their pressure for sweeping measures to
force change in the white-ruled areas. (See Annex
2 for UN resolutions on Southern Africa.) Although
there is growing African emphasis on the need for
the use of force on southern African issues, the
main thrust is still toward broadening sanctions
to include South Africa and Portugal. The number
of countries supporting these additional measures
or the use of force has grown numerically, but
all of the principal Western nations oppose these
measures. (The US would bear the brunt of any
Western contribution to the large naval forces
required for a blockade to support sanctions.)
Throughout the UN system the Africans have introduced southern African issues into almost all
bodies.

Prospects: This process is likely to continue
and to include serious and perhaps sometimes
successful attempts to exclude South Africa from
various UN bodies. However, there is no real
prospect of extended sanctions because of the
British veto.

US Interests: In the UN we have taken the lead
in the establishment of an arms embargo against
South Africa. We also supported a UN resolution
which declared that the situation in Rhodesia had
become a threat to international peace and which
called for the application of mandatory economic
sanctions. Finally, we supported an African
initiative declaring that South Africa had for-

feited its mandate over South West Africa and calling for establishment of a UN administration over that territory.

The main US political interest in southern African issues at the UN is to keep these issues manageable. On the one hand, we seek to maintain a credible stance on racial questions in the eyes of the black African nations, while on the other we attempt to discourage the adoption of unrealistic measures which would damage other US interests in the area and the UN itself. To a considerable degree, US impetus for and support of the UN Security Council's arms embargo on South Africa and its mandatory economic sanctions against Southern Rhodesia were designed to meet these dual aims. The US has also sought, through its posture on southern African issues, to enhance the prospects for support by the 42 African states on other UN issues, for example, on the Chinese representation question.

Other African Reactions

The intensity of the concern of other African states with southern Africa and accordingly with US relations to southern Africa varies considerably. In the long run, our present level of association with southern Africa could gradually alienate the governing elites of some of the African states, mainly in East Africa, and closer association with South Africa could stimulate retaliatory actions of a specific nature in Algeria, Tanzania, and perhaps Zambia (i.e. actions against aircraft landing rights and overflights or US business operations). At the opposite end of the pole, Ivory Coast privately sees South Africa as an important counterweight to communism in Africa, also as a source of profitable trade and possibly aid. It remains to be seen, however, whether Houphouet-Boigny would feel it politically possible openly to support a closer relationship with South Africa. Gabon and Malagasy Republic would tend in varying degrees to follow Ivory Coast. Malawi has already accepted closer relationships with South Africa.

Between the two poles reactions would vary.

The French-speaking states of West and Central
Africa would take very little if any notice of
the nature of our relations with South Africa,
while the English-speaking countries of West
Africa would be concerned but unlikely to react
in concrete steps adverse to the US. The Arab
states of North Africa would support the black
African states, but would be unlikely to take
specific actions beyond verbal admonition. The
English-speaking black states of Kenya and
Uganda in East Africa, would have strong,
verbal, negative reactions to closer US relations with South Africa.

The Organization of African Unity has taken
a strong public position in favor of self-
determination and majority rule in southern
Africa. However, appropriations by member states
of the OAU for the African Liberation Committee
and enthusiasm for the liberation struggle have
recently fallen off.

The Liberation Movements

Although there are eleven identifiable liberation movements operating in southern Africa
(see Annex 5) only three - GRAE in Angola, ZAPU
in Rhodesia and FRELIMO in Mozambique - are con-
ducting significant guerrilla activities. They
receive support from member states of the
Organization of African Unity (OAU) through its
African Liberation Committee (ALC). US public
sympathy for black African national aspirations
and support for refugees have given them moral
encouragement. Principal support from outside
Africa comes from the USSR, Communist China and
Cuba. The Communist powers have not thus far
demonstrated a willingness to become directly
involved in military operations against a white
regime. They probably will continue to supply
military equipment and instructors to the liberation groups and give strong verbal support to
their cause.

In the short term, some increase in activity
by liberation groups and retaliatory measures
by white-regime security forces are likely. However, most liberation groups have had serious
difficulty in recruiting members within the

target countries. There is no likelihood in the foreseeable future that liberation movements could overthrow or seriously threaten the existing white government. Rebel activity may expand and contract from time to time, but there will be no definitive victory or defeat resulting from the guerrilla activities. In Angola and Mozambique, where insurgency is most active, the rebels cannot win militarily - but neither can the Portuguese. In the longer run the most likely prospect is a continuation of present trends - a rise in activity and the number of incidents, but no conclusive results.

There is a wide spectrum of African reaction to and involvement in the liberation struggle, even among the "militants". Nyerere, whose country borders Mozambique, is far more directly concerned and active than are Boumedienne and Sekou Toure 3,000 miles away in Algiers and Conakry. Some of the more conservative African leaders show their distrust of the OAU African Liberation Committee by failing to pay their assessment to its $2 million annual budget. The reaction of Black African leaders must also be considered in terms of the situation and the locale of the discussion. Thus privately a number of African leaders are much more flexible on southern Africa than they can or will be in public - partly because younger elements in the country tend to be more activist on such issues as southern Africa. In the United Nations, however, Africans generally act as a group on these issues, and their public stance is far more extreme. In African councils, the OAU is expected to continue to view the liberation of southern Africa as a - if not the - most important policy of the organization. It will push unity on the liberation factions, and will urge more OAU contributions to the ALC.

The African Manifesto

On April 16, 1969, the Fifth Summit Conference of East and Central African States, a group of fourteen nations, meeting in Lusaka,

Zambia, issued the African Manifesto to explain
the reasons for its hostility to the white minority regimes of southern Africa. This document
is considered to be remarkably articulate and
remarkably restrained.

The signatory nations state that they are
hostile to the regimes not because the regimes
are white or even because they are, at the
moment, minority regimes. The African nations
are hostile because the regimes pursue systematically a doctrine of human inequality denying
human dignity, indeed denying that all human
beings properly are members of the human race.
If change without violence were possible, the
Africans would urge the use of peaceful methods
even if the changes were to take a longer time.
But so long as peaceful progress is blocked by
minority regimes, there is no choice but to
support liberation groups in their struggle.

Since the obstacles to change are not all
the same in southern Africa, the Manifesto also
deals separately with each area: in the Portuguese territories the basic problem is not
racialism but denial of political rights to the
inhabitants of Angola and Mozambique. The fact
of the subjugation of the people of Angola and
Mozambique by Portugal is diametrially opposed
to the ideals and politics of Portugal's allies
(i.e., the US). In the case of Rhodesia, if the
colonial power is unable or unwilling to transfer power to the people of Rhodesia, then the
people must capture it as they can. The avoid-
ance of violence in the settlement of the South
West African problem is the responsibility of
the United Nations. The permanent members of the
Security Council have failed to support UN
actions already taken toward independence. The
Manifesto states that because its apartheid
policy is an offence against humanity, South
Africa should be excluded from the United Nations
and be ostracized by the world community. It
should not be allowed both to reject the very
concept of mankind's unity and to benefit by the
strength given through friendly international
relations.

Other Reactions

Soviet and Chinese Intentions in Southern Africa

Both the USSR and Communist China can be expected to exploit targets of opportunity so long as they are available. They will take every occasion to identify publicly with the cause of the black liberation movements and to present the Western nations as unsympathetic to that cause if not openly in support of continued white control in southern Africa. Both will continue to garner sympathy from most African states for their efforts to aid the liberation movements. They provide arms, training and funds to a variety of liberation movements and would probably provide more if the capacity of these groups to use aid effectively were to grow. They are likely to wish to avoid direct military involvement, however. They probably will continue to funnel much of their support through the African Liberation Committee (ALC) and the Tanzanian government.

The Soviets appear to afford Africa a low priority at present and can be expected to limit the extent of their commitment and involvement. The Chinese Communists, on the other hand, have undertaken a major commitment in East Africa to build a railroad in Zambia and Tanzania apparently in an effort to enhance their influence in these border states of the southern African region. The size of this commitment indicates the intention to increase ChiCom influence in these important host countries for insurgent groups.

UK Interests and Involvement

The UK has historically been heavily involved throughout the region. Despite its contracting overseas commitments, the UK is likely to continue to be a major factor in the area.

Perhaps the overriding UK interest is the importance for her balance of payments of trade, earnings on investment, and other invisibles from South Africa. Investment alone in that country is estimated at $3 billion. This key

interest explains UK reluctance to move deci-
sively on a range of southern African issues,
such as South West Africa where it abstained on
the key UN General Assembly resolution which
determined that South Africa had forfeited its
mandate, or even on Southern Rhodesia where the
UK has indicated it will not support the extension on mandatory economic sanctions to
South Africa and Portugal.

The second key UK interest is its involvement in the rebellion in its Rhodesian colony.
The UK government, while it has several times
sought a negotiated settlement with the Rhodesian authorities on the basis of unimpeded
progress towards majority rule in the colony,
is sensitive to support for its policy by other
foreign powers.

In the black states of the region the main
UK interest is its sizeable equity ownership in
the rich mining facilities of the Zambian copperbelt, the key supply area of this mineral
for the UK market. The UK furnishes budgetary
and developmental support, as well as personnel,
to a number of the black states in the region
and could well have security obligations in
emergencies by virtue of Commonwealth ties.

Other Interests

Other Free World powers having significant
interests in the region include France, Italy,
West Germany, Switzerland and Japan. Most of
these interests relate to trade and investment
but France has a space tracking station and,
despite its formal adherence to the UN arms embargo, sells a broad range of military equipment to South Africa.

US Congressional Reactions

Congress has not thus far demonstrated general interest in southern African questions, but
an increasing number of members are concerned
about our relations with the region. Of interested Senators and Congressmen, the majority
are critical of South Africa (see Annex 6 for a
discussion of Congressional interest).

ANNEXES

Annex 1   (SECRET)   NSC – Southern Africa

POPULATION BREAKDOWN BY COUNTRY AND RACE[1]

	African	% of Total	White	% of Total	Asians & Colored	% of Total	TOTAL[5]
Angola[2]	4.900	95	.270	5	.075	–	5.230
Botswana	.600	100	–	–	–	–	.600
Guinea, Port[2]	.500	100	.002	–	–	–	.500
Lesotho	1.000	100	–	–	–	–	1.000
Malawi	4.000	100	.007	–	.012	–	4.000
Mozambique[2]	7.300	98	.160	2	.045	–	7.505
South Africa[3]	12.700	68	3.600	19	2.400[4]	13	18.700
Southern Rhodesia[5]	4.800	96	.228	4	.023	–	5.051
Southwest Africa	.400	81	.070	14	.020	5	.500
Swaziland	.400	100	.010	–	.010	–	.400
Zambia	3.800	98	.072	2	.010	–	3.900
REGIONAL TOTALS	40.000	85	4.356	9	2.575	6	47.000[6]

1. In thousands (estimates)
2. White population figures do not include Portuguese Military Forces
3. 1967 estimates
4. 1.8 million colored; .6 million Asians
5. March 1969 census
6. Totals rounded – do not exactly equal columnar totals (off 31,000)

Annex 2   Annex to NSC paper on southern Africa

REPRESENTATIVE UN RESOLUTIONS AND
RELATED EXECUTIVE ORDERS ON
SOUTHERN AFRICAN QUESTIONS

A. Apartheid

1. General Assembly Resolution 1761 (XVIII),
   November 6, 1962.

   Action: Requested member states to take
   punitive measures against South Africa as a
   means to induce the Republic to abandon
   apartheid.

   Vote: 67-16-23.

   US Position: No – In the absence of a threat
   to international peace and security, sanctions would be both inappropriate and ineffective.

2. Security Council Resolution 181 (1963),
   August 7, 1963.

   Action: Requested all states to cease the
   sale of arms, ammunition, and military
   vehicles to South Africa.

   Vote: 9-0-2 (UK, France).

   US Position: Yes – South Africa's failure to
   discharge its obligations under Articles 55
   and 56 of the Charter (respect for human

rights and fundamental freedom) called for some concrete demonstration of international concern.

3. Security Council Resolution 182 (1963), December 4, 1963.

   Action: Requested all states to cease the sale of equipment and materials for the manufacture and maintenance of arms and ammunition to South Africa.

   Vote: 11-0-0.

   US Position: Yes - Some further demonstration of international concern about South Africa's social policies was desirable and, in addition, this measure would help to eliminate a factor contributing to international friction.

4. General Assembly Resolution 2396 (XXIII), December 2, 1968.

   Action: Requested member states to take punitive measures against South Africa and to lend moral, political, and material assistance to the South African "liberation movement".

   Vote: 85-2-14.

   US Position: Abstain - In the absence of a threat to international peace and security, sanctions would be both inappropriate and ineffective.

B. Namibia (South West Africa)

1. Security Council Resolution 245 (1968), January 25, 1968.

   Action: Called on South Africa to release and repatriate 37 Namibians being tried on terrorism charges.

   Vote: 15-0-0.

US Position: Yes – South Africa had no legal right to arrest and try the 37 on charges arising out of the Terrorism Act.

2. Security Council Resolution 246 (1968), March 14, 1968.

   Action: Decided to meet again to decide on punitive measures against South Africa if the Republic continued to refuse to comply with Security Council Resolution 245 (1968).

   Vote: 15-0-0.

   US Position: Yes – South Africa's refusal to release and repatriate the 37 would be in defiance of the Security Council.

3. Security Council Resolution 264 (1969), March 20, 1969.

   Action: Called on South Africa to withdraw from Namibia and decided to meet again to decide on punitive measures if the Republic refused to comply.

   Vote: 13-0-2 (UK, France).

   US Position: Yes – South Africa's presence in the territory had been declared to be illegal by the General Assembly.

4. Security Council Resolution of August 12, 1969.

   Action: Called on South Africa to withdraw from Namibia immediately and in any case before October 4, 1969, and decided that in event of failure of South Africa to comply, Security Council will meet immediately to determine effective measures under Charter.

   Vote: 11-0-4 (US, UK, France, Finland).

   US Position: Abstained – US could not accept definitive terminal date with implication of follow-on mandatory measures under Charter.

C. Southern Rhodesia

1. Security Council Resolution 232 (1966),
   December 16, 1966.

   Action: Decided to impose mandatory economic
   sanctions against the illegal Rhodesian regime; embargoed trade in selected items.

   Vote: 15-0-0.

   US Position: Yes - The situation in Southern
   Rhodesia constituted a threat to international peace and security, because racial
   tensions, created by the Smith regime's policies, could result in violent racial conflict
   spreading across international boundaries.
   Short of force, economic sanctions were the
   strongest means of pressure available to the
   international community.

2. Executive Order 11322, January 5, 1967.

   Action: Implemented the mandatory provisions
   of Security Council Resolution 232 (1966) by
   authority of the United Nations Participation
   Act of 1945, as amended.

3. Security Council Resolution 253 (1968),
   May 29, 1968.

   Action: Decided to make the Southern Rhodesian embargo list comprehensive.

   Vote: 15-0-0.

   US Position: Yes - Stepped-up pressure on
   the illegal regime was desirable because
   selective sanctions had not induced Smith to
   come to terms with the UK.

4. Executive Order 11419, July 29, 1968.

   Action: Implemented the mandatory provisions
   of Security Council Resolution 253 (1968).

EFFECT OF SANCTIONS ON
RHODESIAN ECONOMY

UN mandatory sanctions have failed to force the Smith regime to reach an acceptable accommodation with the UK. South African assistance has averted economic disaster. Smith is banking on the prospect that an indefinite continuation of sanctions will result in the erosion of the willingness of nations to enforce the program - even at present levels - and thus bring sanctions to an end.

His analysis is probably correct. There is a growing trend among many of the world's major trading nations to evade or ignore the program. Many UN members have never enforced sanctions as vigorously as have the US and UK; South Africa and Portugal refused to implement them from the beginning.

The man-on-the-street in Rhodesia has not been seriously affected although he has suffered inconveniences. Sanctions have, however, affected regime economic planners and Rhodesian businessmen. The program has constricted the economy and seriously retarded economic growth. Together with rising African unemployment, inflationary pressures and an annual 3½ percent increase in the African population, sanctions have set back the pace of Rhodesia's economic development. Normal trade patterns have been disrupted and trade is carried on under conditions somewhat unfavorable to Rhodesia. It is for these economic reasons that many Rhodesian businessmen have urged Smith to negotiate a settlement and end sanctions. These same individuals are a major force behind the "moderate" opposition's campaign against the regime's proposed constitution and for a settlement which would end sanctions.

Nevertheless, trade is taking place, albeit at only 60 percent of the 1965 level. While 1969 may see the trend reversed, the regime's efforts to raise exports have so far met with no suc-

cess and the value of exports has declined
every year since 1965:

1965	$442	million
1966	$290	million
1967	$282	million
1968	$272.2	million

The regime has encouraged the growth of import substitution industries, subsidized tobacco
farmers and encouraged agricultural diversifi-
cation. These measures have met with some success and the level of economic activity is now
back to 1965 levels. Continued improvement, however, hinges on the regime's ability to expand
export markets and to attract sufficient capital.

Attempts to export more manufactures to South
Africa have resulted in restrictive import quotas
and tariffs on certain items as South African
manufacturers complained of the loss of domestic
markets.

The regime announced a $4.5 million deficit
in the overall balance of payments account for
1968; this compares with a surplus of $9.2 mil-
lion in 1967. Drought and frost contributed to
the deficit through a significant drop in agricultural production; the same conditions will
not be present in 1969. Some $70 million of
capital inflow made up most of what could have
been a disastrous deficit for the regime; the
most likely source of this capital was South
Africa which for obvious reasons does not want
economic sanctions to work; the precedent would
be ominous.

The regime has faced a recurring and trouble-
some shortage of foreign exhange which caused
serious difficulties during the last quarter of
1968. The tobacco industry, pre-UDI's major
foreign exchange earner, has been hard hit; the
American tobacco industry has taken over Rhodesia's share of the British market and now
supplies half of the UK's tabacco imports. Imports have been subjected to a cutback of at
least 4 percent each quarter since August 1968.
The South Africans have also made loans which
have helped ease the pressure. The first half of
1969 will be a period of some strain on Rho-

146

desia's external payments account and imports
will likely be held to a minimum. (The Rhodesians have informed us that unless some funds
can be unblocked from suspended London accounts,
they may not be able to pay the annual instal-
ment on the 1954 AID railway loan.) However, if
the present increase in sanctions evasion continues, the pressures should ease during the
last half of this year.

The isolation and "state of siege" feeling
has help solidify white support for the regime;
Smith, himself, enjoys great personal popularity
among the majority of the white electorate.
Smith recognizes, however, that psychological
and economic requirements over the long haul
dictate ending the present political ostracism
and economic isolation in which Rhodesia finds
itself and stresses that adoption of the new
constitution and republican states for Rhodesia
will enable "friendly" nations to trade more
openly and recognize Rhodesian independence.

US trade with Rhodesia has always been a very
small factor in our world wide totals. Total
trade amounted to some $33 million in 1965; our
enforcement of sanctions reduced this amount to
$3.7 million in 1968 and the total should drop
even further in 1969 as the comprehensive embargo takes effect.

US present book value of investment in the
territory, too, is miniscule when compared with
other countries. In 1967, total US investment
amounted to $56 million; this contrasts to some
$100 million in neighboring black-ruled Zambia
(primarily copper) and some $125 million in
Angola (oil).

The program has adversely affected certain
US companies who have chrome mining interests
in Rhodesia. Along with South Africa, Turkey
and the USSR, Southern Rhodesia is a major
source of metallurgical chromite. With sanctions,
American companies have not been able to utilize
their mines, and our imports of metallurgical
chrome from the USSR have risen; this situation
has led to some Congressional criticism.

The US is not, however, completely dependent
on the Soviets for metallurgical chromite and
while the Soviet share of American market has

risen, absolute quantities have remained relatively stable as the following chart indicates:

Imports of Chromite from USSR and
Southern Rhodesia for Metallurgical Use[1]

	1963	1964	1965	1966	1967	1968
Total Imports	564	828	884	913	660	585
From S. Rhodesia and % of total	272(48%)	346(42%)	329(37%)	219(24%)	147(22%)	1(-%)
From USSR and % of total	192(34%)	297(36%)	242(27%)	302(33%)	299(45%)	335(37%)

1. In thousands of short tons

Annex 4   NSC – Southern Africa

RHODESIAN CHROME ORE AND SANCTIONS

Problem: Union Carbide and Foote Mineral own
chrome ore mines in Southern Rhodesia. They want
to import 207,000 tons of chrome ore produced
in those mines. The ore in question is metallurgical chromite, the major sources for which
are limited to the Soviet Union, Turkey and
Southern Rhodesia. Companies claim they paid
for the ore in question either before sanctions,
or afterwards with the permission of the USG;
therefore, it is alleged that no further economic benefit would accrue to Rhodesia if the
chrome were now to be exported. None of the
chrome was exported from Rhodesia before mandatory sanctions took effect.

There is a distinction between the Carbide and
Foote cases, however. Carbide claims its 150,000
tons were mined before the imposition of mandatory sanctions and were paid for on December 21,
1966, before the issuance of the Executive Order
on January 5, 1967. Carbide also claims that
some of the ore would have been exported prior
to sanctions if the company had not cooperated
with the USG during the period of "voluntary
sanctions" in 1966. Foote's 57,000 tons, on the
other hand, were mined in 1967 and 1968 with
funds legally transferred on the basis of the
company's claim that the mines had to be worked
at a minimum level to avoid flooding and irre-
trievable loss. The funds were transferred with
the permission of the USG with the explicit
understanding that the resulting production
could not be licensed for import into the US. By
the end of 1967, Foote had determined it could
no longer maintain the mine without having access to the ore and ceased transferring funds.
In January 1968 the regime put Foote's Rhodesian
mine under mandate and assumed the operating
expenses.

UN resolutions prohibit imports of chrome by
member states exported from Rhodesia after December 16, 1966. US Executive Order of January
5, 1967 implementing the first Resolution im-

poses the same prohibition notwithstanding prior contracts.

A Treasury press release accompanying issuance of sanctions regulations on March 1, 1967, states licenses would be given for goods exported from Rhodesia prior to December 16, 1966 and, on the basis of undue hardship, "in general" would be given for goods paid for but not exported before January 5, 1967. While Foote's application meets neither of the criteria, Carbide's application meets the second. In strictly legal terms, however, both purchases fall under the prohibitions of the Executive Order and clearly violate the intent of the UN resolution.

Certain columnists, pressure groups, pro-Rhodesian/South African organizations, some domestic ferroalloy producers and certain members of Congress are urging that the importation of Rhodesian chrome be permitted.

Question: Should we license the importation into the US of these 207,000 tons of Rhodesian chrome?

PROS:

1. Would aid the two American firms by giving them access to their chrome ore for which they have already expended funds.
2. Would show the American business community that the USG endeavors to support US business interests.
3. Would ease pressure on the tightening chrome supply in US.
4. Would help reduce growing dependence on Soviet Union as principal source of metallurgical chromite for the next twelve months.
5. Would not provide an economic benefit to Rhodesia because US dollars have already been spent.
6. Would enable Administration to take favorable action in response to strong pressures.
7. Case might be made that we are hurting rather than helping the regime, viz, by removing an asset which Rhodesians might otherwise expropriate and sell on black market to obtain badly needed foreign exchange.

8. Importation of the ore would be in accord with strategic requirements.
9. It would be only a one-time action.
10. Some benefit to overall balance of payments.

CONS:

1. Only two American firms would be given access to the chrome. One other US firm (Metallurg, an American corporation, incorporated in New York) also owns chrome interests in Rhodesia and might attempt to claim similar disadvantage and apply for relief.
2. Importers of other Rhodesian goods (asbestos, lithium, nickel) would be encouraged to apply for licenses to import from former Rhodesian sources; pressures to end sanctions restrictions would increase.
3. The chrome ore supply situation is tight, but not critical. No problem is anticipated in meeting US requirements in the next year or two. Ore is still available in various quantities for 1969 contract delivery from Turkey, Iran, India and Pakistan as well as from the USSR.
4. Members of Congress and US groups supporting the UN sanctions against Southern Rhodesia are likely to criticize the action vehemently as "giving in" to the racist Smith regime for purely economic reasons.
5. Rhodesians are unable to sell all present chrome inventory; one million tons presently stockpiled. Even if Smith regime expropriated these 207,000 tons, it would have difficulty in disposing of them quickly, particularly the 57,000 tons of fines and concentrates produced by Foote.
6. US relationship with UK would be adversely affected over the Rhodesian issue - we have consistently supported the UK on Rhodesia and the UK undoubtedly would look upon importation of the ore as a backing away from that support.
7. Although the action might be explained on hardship grounds under the Treasury press release, it would contravene the UN Resolution and Executive Order which specifically prohi-

bit imports of chrome exported from Rhodesia after December 15, 1966, notwithstanding any prior contracts.

8. Reaction of most UN members, as well as reaction in Africa and elsewhere, would be to read the US action as a lessening of support for the UN, an open violation of a mandatory provision of the sanctions resolution and as a change in US policy.

9. In some cases, it would encourage other nations to drop sanctions against Rhodesia or at least weaken their enforcement of this program.

10. US sincerity in its avowed support for self-determination in Rhodesia would be questioned by some and our influence with many African States reduced.

11. The political benefits would be a wind-fall for Smith and subsequent concrete economic benefits might accrue to the regime as willingness to enforce the sanctions was eroded.

12. Licensing the 207,000 tons solves neither long-range chrome supply problem nor would it free US industry from continuing purchases from USSR - even were sanctions to be ended, substantial quantities of chrome would continue to be imported from the USSR.

SECRET - NO FOREIGN DISSEM

Annex 5

LIBERATION GROUPS OF SOUTHERN AFRICA

Angola

1. GRAE. The Angolan Revolutionary Government in Exile, probably still the largest of the Angolan movements, is an outgrowth of political groups formed in the mid-1950's and partly responsible for the start of the insurgency in 1961. GRAE is dominated by Holden Roberto and draws the great bulk of its active members from his fellow Bakongo tribesmen. Most of its external support is from moderate African states.

Congo (Kinshasa) serves as political headquarters and as the training and staging base
for GRAE insurgents. Guerrilla groups have been
persistently active in northwest Angola since
1961. Over the past two years GRAE has also
engaged in sporadic guerrilla incursions along
the central and eastern sectors of the Congo-
Angola border.

2. MPLA. The Popular Movement for the Liberation of Angola was organized in the mid-1950's
by urban blacks and mulattoes and has taken
part in the insurgency since 1961. It is led by
Angostinho Neto. Based for a long time in Congo
(Brazzaville), it now operated principally out
of Dar es Salaam through Zambia. It espouses a
pro-Communist line and draws most of its financial and military assistance from the USSR, although since moving to Tanzania it may have
received at least indirect assistance from Communist China. Its guerrilla activities in
northwest Angola and the Cabinda enclave are
insubstantial, but it has some political cells
in Luanda and other non-insurgent areas. Its
operations from Zambia against eastern Angola,
began in 1966, are rated by the Portuguese as
the most effective guerrilla force they face.

3. UNITA. The National Union for the Total
Liberation of Angola was formed in 1966 by Jonas
Savimbi, a defector from GRAE. It has a small
core of trained guerrillas and at one time had
gained the support, through tribal affinity, of
a number of villages in eastern and central
Angola. Savimbi was obliged to leave Zambia in
1967 and, after living in Cairo for some time,
reportedly returned to Angola some time in 1968.
Although UNITA has received minor Chinese military and financial aid it has greater logistic
problems than the other movements and has
recently declined.

Mozambique

1. FRELIMO. The Mozambique Liberation Front
springs from dissident groups organized in the
early 1960's and began its insurgency in 1964.

153

It is led by Uria Simimgo who was named Acting
President after the assassination of Eduardo
Mondlane. A large number of its 6,000 to 8,000
trained fighters are from the Maconde tribe of
northern Mozambique, the area of its querrilla
operations. FRELIMO has headquarters in Tanzania,
the staging base for its guerrilla incursions.
It receives most of its external financial aid
from African sources. The USSR and China both
provide military assistance. FRELIMO guerrilla
tactics have grown increasingly proficient, but
the Portuguese have somewhat reduced the area of
their operations on the north over the past year
at the same time as FRELIMO opened a new, but
smaller, front on the western border with Zambia.
The assassination of Mondlane was followed a
short time later by the defection to the Portuguese of a Maconde tribal leader who has urged
his fellow tribesmen to lay down their arms.
It is unlikely that these setbacks presage
FRELIMO's demise but it is too early to assess
their effect on the organization.

2. <u>COREMO.</u> The Mozambique Revolutionary Committee split off from FRELIMO in 1964. Zambia-
based, it suffers from internal dissension although it sporadically ventures into western
Mozambique for political activity and occasionally for guerrilla raids. Led by Paula
Gumane, it has at the most 100 to 200 members
and receives an occasional flow of small-scale
assistance from China.

Rhodesia

1. <u>ZAPU.</u> The Zimbabwe African Peoples Union,
successor to earlier nationalist parties, was
formed in 1961 and banned in 1962. Its best
known leaders, including President Joshua Nkomo,
and many members are under detention. Its active
members are mostly in exile, led by Acting
President James Chikerema. Political headquarters are in Zambia, which permits border cross-
ings by guerrillas, but not the use of its
territory for training. Military training takes
place in Tanzania, Cuba, Algeria, USSR and other
countries. Most of ZAPU's financial support

comes from African states; some funds and most
of its military equipment from the USSR, via the
OAU's African Liberation Committee. ZAPU has
made serious efforts to infiltrate guerrillas
into Rhodesia, and some fairly large groups
(100-200 men each) have crossed the border, but
the overwhelming majority have been killed or
captured or have deserted. The ZAPU organization
within Rhodesia has been badly damaged, perhaps
crippled, by infiltrations and arrests by
security forces.

2. ZANU. The Zimbabwe African National Union
was formed in 1963, with the defection of a
group of urban intellectuals from ZAPU. ZANU was
banned in 1964 and its leaders, including President Ndabaninge Sithole, arrested. It now is
led by Acting President Herbert Chitepo and
probably is smaller than ZAPU, its bitter rival.
It, too, is based in Zambia and receives military training in Tanzania, as well as other
countries. Communist China has supplied small
amounts of military and financial aid, and some
training. ZANU's efforts to mount guerrilla warfare and political activity inside Rhodesian
have been ineffective.

South Africa

1. ANC. The African National Congress was
organized in 1912 and banned in 1960. Many experienced leaders and non-communist members are
under detention. Oliver Tambo now is President.
The ANC is closely associated with the banned
South African Communist Party. Most of its
financial aid is from the Communist Party of
the UK and from the USSR; the latter probably
provides the bulk of its military equipment. The
ANC has headquarters in Tanzania. In addition to
several hundred political exiles scattered
throughout the world, it probably has a hundred
or so trained guerrillas. Occasional attempts to
infiltrate South Africa have been unsuccessful.
Its political organization within the Republic
is weak and infiltrated by government agents.

2. PAC. The Pan-African Congress split off

from the ANC in 1959, because of dissatisfaction with the latter's multiracial character and the extent of Communist influence. It was banned in 1960, with many leaders and members placed under detention. The PAC is wracked by factionalism and probably has no more than 100 or so active members, nearly all in exile. Political headquarters are in Tanzania. China has provided limited financial and military aid.

South West Africa

1. SWAPO. The South West Africa People's Organization, formed in 1959, has perhaps several thousand active members, mostly from the Ovambo, the largest tribe. A minority of SWAPO members, perhaps 200 or so, advocate the use of violence. Led by Sam Nujoma, these have headquarters in Tanzania and receive financial help from a variety of African sources. The USSR provides both monetary and military aid. During 1966-1967, SWAPO guerrilla bands infiltrated SWA, received some local support, and conducted a short-lived guerrilla campaign. This led to a stern crackdown by the South African Government.

2. SWANU. The South West Africa National Union is one of several insubstantial liberation groups formed by dissident Herero tribesmen. It has headquarters in Tanzania but only a miniscule membership.

CONFIDENTIAL

Annex 6

Appendix to Response to NSSM-39
Subject:
GROWING CONGRESSIONAL INTEREST IN
SOUTHERN AFRICA

General

Although Congress as a whole does not show substantial interest in southern Africa, an increasing number of Congressmen and Senators are concerned about our relations, particularly with South Africa, and are willing to support

resolutions or inquiries about US policy. The
large majority of those interested are critical
of South Africa, and some favor extensive disengagement. A minority, not exclusively but
mainly from the South, favor closer relations
with South Africa and a more friendly attitude
toward the Smith regime in Southern Rhodesia.

Insertions in the Congressional Record by
both sides are becoming frequent. They show a
definite linkage of the southern Africa issue
with the civil rights problem in the US. Persons
sensitive to the US aspect are also likely to be
concerned about southern Africa as part of the
universal problem of human rights and dignity.
Their opponents resist this attitude re both the
US and southern Africa. The Congressional study
group on Africa, which is advised by Prof.
Vernon McKay of the John Hopkins School of Advanced International Studies, has focussed some
Congressional attention on the region.

Congressman Charles C. Diggs, Chairman of the
House Subcommittee on Africa, has shown particular interest in Southern Africa and proposes to
move on to a general review of US policy after
hearings on the US-South Africa Air Transport
Agreement and the South African sugar quota.
Congressmen Diggs and Ogden R. Reid planned to
visit South Africa during August 1969, but cancelled their respective visits when informed by
the South African Government that issuance of
visas would be conditional on their not making
speeches during the visits.

Additional efforts to increase Congressional
awareness of African problems have been made by
the New York-based American Committee on Africa
which now has an office in Washington.

US-South African Air Transport Agreement Hearings

Congressman Diggs, Chairman of the Subcommittee on Africa of the House Foreign Affairs Committee, on April 2, 1969 conducted a hearing on
the new South African air route to New York City
via Rio. He strongly protested against the grant
of the route as inconsistent with our relationships with independent black African states and
as a defiance of the UNGA's 1962 resolution re-

157

fusing landing and passage rights to South
Africa (the US voted against the 1962 resolution). Several members of the subcommittee,
including Congressmen Conyers, Culver, Morse
and Rosenthal, supported his view.

Sugar Quota Bills

Senator Edward Kennedy, with 11 other Senators of both parties, and Congressman Jonathan
Bingham, with 22 co-sponsors, including one
Republican - Ogden Reid of New York - introduced
identical bills on April 17 and 18, 1969, to
terminate South Africa's sugar quota. Congressman Bingham proposed the action as a first step
of "prompt disengagement" from our remaining
public and private ties with South Africa.
Senator Kennedy said in the Senate that the time
"is now ripe to begin a reassessment of our
over-all policy toward South Africa." Their
action followed a hearing of the Diggs subcommittee on the subject on April 15. Whatever the
fate of these bills, the US Sugar Act of 1965 is
to be reviewed in Congress by 1971, when its
renewal will be decided.
The sponsors of the respective bills are:

<u>Senators:</u> Kennedy, Brooke, Cranston, Goodell,
Hart, Javits, Mondale, Mundt, Pell, Scott,
Williams (N.J.), Young (Ohio).

<u>Representatives:</u> Brown (Cal.), Clay, Culver,
Diggs, Dulski, Edwards (Cal.), Farbstein,
Fraser, Green (Penn.), Kastenmeier, Roch,
Lowenstein (N.Y.), Mikva, Ottinger, Podell,
Reid (N.Y.), Rodino, Rosenthal, Ryan, St.
Germain, Scheuer, Tiernan.

Ship Visits

In February 1967, when the carrier <u>Roosevelt</u>
was about to refuel at Cape Town enroute to
Vietnam, some 38 Congressmen protested exposure
of Americans to apartheid and shore leaves were
cancelled. On April 21, 1969 Congressman Rosenthal, with 32 Congressmen cosigners, sent a

letter to Secretary Rogers asking whether the
new Administration would continue the practice
of having all Navy ships avoid South African
harbors except in emergency, and whether the
policy long "under review" would be decided soon
or delayed. Of the 33 signers, 28 were among the
38 who protested the visit of the FDR.

Congressional Mail

Letters from Congressmen to the Department
and letters to them referred to the Department
are generally topical - on current issues such
as the South African air route to New York
City, the Sugar Act quota, trials and prison
torture, and visa-passport problems. Hardy
perennials are the space facilities in South
Africa, US investment and trade, and the lack
of American negroes in our Embassy and Consulates in South Africa. The volume is generally small, but a dramatic incident or a
campaign by the American Committee on Africa
or the Episcopal Churchmen for South Africa,
both organizations located in New York City,
can occasion a flurry of letters resulting
from meetings and mail appeals for protest
action.

(SECRET)

Annex 7

Submitted to AF/NSC-IG by
AID, June 9, 1969.

CONSIDERATIONS INVOLVED IN ESTABLISHMENT
OF SIGNIFICANT BILATERAL ASSISTANCE
FOR THE BLACK STATES OF SOUTHERN AFRICA
(Zambia, Malawi, Botswana, Lesotho and Swaziland)

Our current aid policy toward Africa limits
bilateral AID programs to selected "emphasis"
countries (now ten in number) and provides US
assistance in all other countries through AID
regional and multi-donor projects, PL 480, Peace
Corps., and investment guarantees. For this reason and because of funding and staff limitations,
the resumption or initiation of bilateral AID
programs becomes a key issue.

PROS:

This US action could be an element of any of the options in this paper, although its weight in each approach might vary. The action would aim at the development of the economic and political independence of the black states bordering on and surrounded by the white minority regimes. Some of these states capable of developing successful non-racial societies are hostages to South Africa for economic and technical assistance. Others with a high economic potential are seeking help from any quarter of the outside world. The goal of the US would be to serve as an alternative not only to South Africa but also to mainland China and Russia. The prospect of a predominantly white society (the US) assisting predominantly black societies to escape domination by white minority regimes (primarily South Africa) might help depolarize the racial element of the confrontation in southern Africa.

Under this course of action, the US would provide aid programs that would include technical assistance, thus possibly reducing present reliance on South African technicians, and also financing for the development of institutions and infrastructure. We would be receptive to the needs expressed by the five countries. The US would consider favorably requests for defensive armament. We would continue to seek amendment of Conte legislation to ease present restrictions. We would make a determined effort to encourage other countries and international organizations to make greater contributions to development in southern Africa, and encourage multi-donor projects.

US assistance could have the following favorable aspects:

1. Significant bilateral assistance by the US could give us effective influence on the attitudes of these states.
2. Concrete manifestations of the concern of the US for the welfare of these states could depolarize the racial aspect of the southern African confrontation and perhaps inhibit

exploitation by the white minority regimes.
At the same time the US might be able to influence the orderly and prosperous development of multi-racial societies in those
states where a potential exists.

The impact of the foregoing US actions over
the next three to five years can be estimated
as follows:

US aid to Zambia, Malawi, Botswana, Lesotho,
and Swaziland would not be a major solution
to Southern Africa's problems. It could, however, give us some additional influence with
those states, and might help to focus their
attention on their internal problems. It
would not eliminate the basic racial tensions
in the area, although by providing an alternative to dependence on the white states it
might moderate these tensions somewhat.

CONS:

The question of bilateral aid must be considered in the perspective of:

(a) US interests in each country as well as
in the region as a whole: in both absolute
and relative terms, these interests are
limited, except possibly in Zambia because of
US investments;
(b) the nature, volume, and significance of
US bilateral and regional programs in each
country and the possibilities for expanding
such programs under current policy; (A statement of our aid activities in each country is
attached. Although the Conte problem in Zambia has limited our activities, if the legislation is amended as proposed, the potential
for regional projects involving Zambia would
increase measurably.)
(c) the very important differences between
the several countries in terms of size (and
population), economic potential, other donor
assistance programs, relations with and economic and political dependence on the white
regimes: only Zambia and Botswana have

demonstrated that they want to reduce their dependence on the white redoubts; both countries have economic potential and both have access to outside, non-SAG assistance; Swaziland has some economic resources, but is willingly in the SAG orbit as are Lesotho and Malawi, neither of which have much economic potential.

It can be argued that the only benefits to be derived from bilateral AID programs are psychological and that it is doubtful that any but massive economic assistance <u>could</u> (not <u>would</u>) achieve the desired political objectives. On the contrary, new bilateral programs could (a) vitiate efforts to encourage constructive relationships between the black states and their white neighbors, (b) add to hopes for the impossible in terms of US political and economic involvement, and (c) lead to British efforts to reduce their financial assistance or to British objections where US aid necessitates increases in budget support.

Present and immediately foreseeable levels of AID assistance for Africa (and BALPA staff ceilings) are likely to permit only "presence" type programs which could accomplish no greater results than can be achieved through an active and imaginative resort to the regional and multi-donor AID instruments as well as non-AID bilateral instruments, which permit such politically visible activities as the Shashi development in Botswana, the Tan Zam Highway benefiting Zambia, large scale food aid and the prospective Oxbow project in Lesotho, moderate sized Peace Corps contingents in four countries, refugee education, faculty help to UBLS, scholarship programs, and high impact Self-Help projects. The large capital assistance projects being financed in Zambia by the IBRD with USG encouragement offsets in some measure the limitations on our ability to aid that country directly. And more can be done by the USG to support increased IBRD, UN, and other donor help for the area.

Finally, the resumption or initiation of bilateral AID programs must be considered in the light of Congressional attitudes. This action

162

would constitute a major change in US aid policy toward Africa as presented to Congress. The changes would have to be discussed with the interested Committees, three of which are chaired by Members likely to be critical of what might be described as a use of AID programs to become more deeply involved in the confrontation between the white-ruled countries and the neighboring black nations.

Even if Congressional approval could be obtained without damage to our overall program, no increase in funds would be forthcoming in FY 1970 and probably not in FY 1971. Under these circumstances, we would have to spread our limited resources over more countries, thereby penalizing the more important African countries and our regional and multi-donor projects, reducing the effectiveness of aid in development terms. In view of the sustained decline in US aid to Africa over the past several years, this might possibly lead to a deterioration in our relations with other African states.

US ASSISTANCE IN SOUTHERN* AFRICA SINCE FY 1965

	1965–1968	FY 1969 Estimate ($ Million)	FY 1970 Request
Zambia			
AID	4.0	–	0.1
PL 480	0.2	–	–
World Bank (IBRD)	21.3	32.0	N.A.
UN	8.5	1.5[6]	N.A.
Malawi			
AID	13.4	1.2	0.1
PL 480	0.1	0.1	0.1
PC (Approx. No. PCV's)	450[1]	145[2]	155
World Bank (IDA)	27.5	–	N.A.
UN	4.6	0.8[6]	N.A.
Botswana			
AID	0.2	0.1	7.1

PL 480	17.3	–	–
PC (Approx. No. PCV's)	110[1]	70[2]	88[3]
World Bank (IDA)	3.6	–	35–45
UN	2.3	0.6[6]	N.A.
Lesotho			
AID	0.3	0.1	0.1
PL 480	2.3	0.8	0.5
PC (Approx. No. PCV's)	70[1]	57[2]	85[3]
World Hank (IDA)	4.1	–	N.A.
UN	0.8	1.8[6]	N.A.
Swaziland			
AID	–	0.1	0.1
PL 480	Neg.	Neg.	Neg.
PC (Approx. No. PCV's)	47[1]	44[2]	43[3]
World Bank (IBRD)	2.8	–	N.A.
UN	2.3	0.2[6]	N.A.
Regional (AID)			
Refugee Education	5.3	0.7	0.6
Great North Road (Zambia – Tanzania)	13.0	6.5	–
AHEP, ASPAU, AFRGRAD	114	55[5]	N.A.
UBLS (Botswana, Lesotho, Swaziland)	0.4	0.4	0.2
SA Testing Center (Malawi, Botswana, Lesotho, Swaziland)	–	0.3	0.3
Teacher Education for East Africa (Zambia)	0.2	**	0.3
Teacher Education for Southern Africa (Botswana, Lesotho, Swaziland, Malawi)	–	–	0.3
Zambia – Botswana Transport Survey	–	0.2	–[2]
SA Regional Techni-			

cal Training (Malawi,
Botswana, Lesotho,
Swaziland)   —   —   0.1

*US contributions to International programs are
 IBRD — 28%, IDA — 32% and UN — 40%.
**Less than $50,000.

1. Estimated cost; Malawi $4.7; Botswana $1.0 mn.;
   Lesotho $0.6 mn.; Swaziland $0.2 mn.
2. In country at present.
3. Program memorandum targets for 6/30/70.
4. Loan for final engineering possible in
   FY 1970.
5. New starts in current year.
6. Small additional "other" amount not included
   since not yet available.

CONFIDENTIAL

Annex 8

Submitted to AF/NSC-IG by
NASA, July 22, 1969

US NATIONAL SPACE PROGRAM
RELIANCE ON SOUTH AFRICA

General

    The NASA unmanned planetary exploration
spacecraft, as they have in the past, must continue to depend heavily upon the tracking
station located in South Africa in achieving
mission success. The importance of ground instrumentation support from this geographical
area arises simply from the fact that it is
uniquely located in the "key hole" view of almost all missions launched from Cape Kennedy,
Florida. Launch trajectories of these planetary
bound missions are such that flight events which
are critical to mission success, are viewed by
this first major land mass overflown after
launch and for which vital spacecraft reception
and command information is required. All NASA
planetary missions have relied on the vital
early tracking data information from the South

165

Africa station to provide the extremely critical computations for correcting the trajectory of the spacecraft on the way to the target planet.

In addition to the above important ground tracking function which must be performed for automated planetary space missions, execution of the follow-on Apollo program manned missions also requires support by specially instrumented aircraft (Apollo/Range Instrumentation Aircraft) for critical launch, orbit and recovery phases. Serious constraints on opportunities for injection into earth escape trajectories would occur on certain missions if the aircraft could not stage from Jan Smuts airfield and overfly South Africa in support of these manned missions.

Planetary Program Support Considerations

The South African NASA tracking facility is a vital element in a global network of stations which provides the total communication link with our planetary-bound flight spacecraft. These stations perform three basic functions necessary to mission success tracking – the determination of the precise position and speed of the spacecraft; data acquisition – the reception of information on both scientific experiments and spacecraft "health"; and command and control – the transmission of radio signals to the spacecraft to provide the many instructions necessary in the performance of the flight mission.

The NASA station was located at South Africa both because it had the proper geographic location in relation to the other stations of the Deep Space Network (which are spaced 120^0 apart) and because it is uniquely located to allow the precise tracking of Cape Kennedy-launched spacecraft during the critical phase just after the spacecraft are placed into planetary bound trajectories (post-injection phase). The tracking information obtained during this phase is used to determine the exact midcourse corrections to be made to the spacecraft's flight path in order to achieve ultimate planetary intercept. While trajectory paths will vary somewhat with each mission, the South Africa station is optimumly located to perform this task for all missions.

As the complexity of NASA's Planetary Programs increase by such new missions as the dual orbital spacecraft of the planet Mars in 1971 and a flyby spacecraft of the more distant planet Jupiter in 1972, even greater tracking precision will be required. Thus, the South African station will play even more of a key role during the critical early post-injection phase.

In addition to its unique launch support role, the South African station also is located to operate in conjunction with other deep space stations around the globe to assure continuous communication to spacecraft. During certain periods the planet positions in the ecliptic plane become quite southerly, as in the case for the Mars missions in 1969 and 1971 and Jupiter in 1972. Spacecraft flying to the planets during these periods usually depart from earth in a far southerly trajectory. As a result, for a period of a few months they are viewed primarily by only the Southern Hemisphere stations, South Africa and Australia, both of which are essential to achieve adequate ground tracking, data acquisition, and command support.

Therefore non-availability of the South Africa station would impose serious mission operational constraints and would degrade ground tracking support to a high risk condition. While each planned mission would require a separate detailed analysis, the general magnitude of the effects can be stated as below.

For every 2 year opportunity to achieve a Mars intercept, there exists only a short period of about 30 days during which one can launch (the launch window), with daily opportunity varying from seconds to a few minutes for any specific launch direction. The limitations on this launch window represent a very severe operational constraint.

Unlike the great majority of earth orbiting satellites, for these planetary missions the problem of launch aiming is extremely complicated and must be calculated with exceptionally great precision. The South Africa station is a key factor in achieving a reasonable launch window period, to insure that the planetary opportunity is not missed. In a typical situation, such as the dual spacecraft Mariner Mars 1971 mission, a substantial one-fourth of the total launch window is virtually rendered useless without the availability of tracking support from the South Africa station; since the low inclination of the spacecraft results in a several hour gap in ground communications. During the early period of the launch window this gap is as much as 6 hours daily, i.e., the period during which little or no contact is maintained with the spacecraft. The complexity of these spacecraft, and the precision with which navigation corrections must be made, require that continuous serveillance from the ground be maintained. Past experience with several missions, including Mariner II, Mariner IV, Lunar Orbiter I, Surveyor V, Pioneer VI, VII, and VIII has demonstrated that only with continuous surveillance can malfunctions be detected, and corrected with reliability and in time to insure against loss of the entire spacecraft mission. The dual Mariner 1969 mission during the 70-90 days of its trajectory toward Mars relied solely on the South Africa station for several hours each day.

The above constraints have been considered largely with respect to a "direct-ascent" launch, i.e., one in which the spacecraft uses single, continuous burn, and is aimed from launch at the point of injection into solar orbit. In this mode the correction capability of the spacecraft is extremely small with respect to the errors that can occur if the injection point into solar orbit is missed, either by launch timing or by some anomaly in trajectory. Therefore, in order to expand the inherently narrow window, and to achieve greater precision in trajectory pointing, a dependence has been placed on the "parking orbit" mode. In this mode the spacecraft needs to be aimed initially for injection into earth orbit, with significant reduction in accuracy requirement, and a considerable increase in launch window. Here, again, because of the southeasterly launch corridor out of Cape Kennedy, major coverage during injection out of the low parking orbit occurs in general over the South Africa region. In almost all cases, loss of coverage from this region inhibits the daily launch window by a major amount (at least 50%), which in many cases virtually eliminates the option to utilize this mode. Based on past experience and planned projected mission characteristics, the parking orbit option can as much as double the launch opportunity window period. For example, the Mariner Mars 1969 launch window approximated some 60 days, with heavy and unique dependence on South Africa coverage during the early and mid-mission phases.

Alternatives

NASA, on an urgent basis and at significant expense, has implemented, where feasible, contingency ground tracking facilities. These, however, offer at best only a compromise solution to providing an alternative location to South Africa. This is because, as discussed above, the geographical location of the extreme southern African region, with respect to the flight paths followed out of Cape Kennedy, provide a unique location for the monitoring of planetary bound missions.

To retain the needed geographical location features of this station, construction would have to be initiated in an adjacent black-ruled country. Conservative estimates indicate the cost to be in excess of $35 million dollars for station construction alone, and an increase in operations costs over South Africa of approximately $2.5 million annually. Apart from the high costs, and questions as to political feasibility, NASA considers such action would be highly difficult and undesirable, from the viewpoint of technical implementation, operations, and logistic support, since in such an extremely undeveloped country all technical and community services, communications, and other support would have to be provided from the US.

Summary

To summarize, South Africa provides the geographical location which is unique to and opti-
mum for the launch complex at Cape Kennedy. The
NASA Deep Space Station at this location makes
it possible to achieve the required capability
and flexibility in launch direction and opportunity, and to provide continuous communications
with planetary program spacecraft during all
critical phases of the mission. The impact on
the orderly technical planning for planetary
exploration is obvious should there be a failure to meet any single planned launch opportunity (Mars opportunities, for example, occur
about every 2 years; the span between multiple
outer planetary intercepts is many, many years).
It is considered essential to mission success
to provide a continuous contact capability to
identify and correct deficiencies in trajectory
and spacecraft systems performance. With any
gap in ground communications coverage the risk
of malfunctions is increased and corrective
actions become less effective, or are nullified.
The inability to maintain this continuous contact during critical phases provides an excel-
lent opportunity for the loss of the total
spacecraft mission. The costs of some of the
approved mission spacecraft are approximated to
be $125 million for the Mariner Mars 1969, $120
million for the Mariner Mars 1971, and some
$400 million for the Viking orbiter and lander
mission to Mars in 1973. Additional spacecraft
now approved and under design or fabrication
bring this total up to almost one billion
dollars.

Submitted to AF/NSC - IG by
Department of Commerce
Aug. 5, 1969

US EXPORTS TO AFRICA AND THE
SOUTHERN AFRICA SUB-REGION, *1968
(IN DOLLARS)

Country of Destination	Exports	% of US Exports to Africa	% of total US Exports
Morocco	$ 69,966,322	5.8%	.21%
Algeria	52,839,074	4.4	.16
Tunisia	48,483,679	4.0	.14
Libya	113,770,135	9.5	.33
Sudan	6,219,813	.5	.02
Spanish Africa, N.E.C.	1,165,001	.1	
Mauritania	5,198,829	.4	.02
Federal Republic of Cameroon	10,217,684	.9	.03
Senegal	6,625,801	.6	.02
Guinea	5,759,804	.5	.02
Sierra Leone	6,962,078	.6	.02
Ivory Coast	12,404,191	1.0	.04
Ghana	55,945,197	4.7	.16
Gambia	724,421	.06	
Togo	1,742,412	.1	.01
Nigeria	56,153,397	4.7	.17
Central African Republic	378,062	.03	
Gabon	4,305,979	.4	.01
Western Africa, N.E.C.	10,676,316	.9	.03
British West Africa	53,897		
Western Portuguese Africa, N.E.C.	2,759,654	.2	.01
Liberia	33,375,953	3.2	.11
Congo (K)	50,658,154	4.2	.15
Burundi and Rwanda	2,141,878	.2	.01
Somali Republic	3,822,481	.3	.01
Ethiopia	46,289,222	3.9	.14
Afar and Issas (French)	1,216,691	.1	

Uganda	3,424,641	.3	.01
Kenya	19,685,474	1.6	.06
Seychelles and Dependencies	137,726	.01	
Tanzania	12,858,603	1.1	.04
Mauritius and Dependencies	1,075,014	.08	
Malagasy Republic	5,976,779	.5	.02
Angola	36,665,312	3.1	.11
Mozambique	15,169,826	1.3	.04
Republic of South Africa	453,539,622	37.8	1.33
Zambia	29,777,678	2.5	.09
Rhodesia	2,050,039	.2	.01
Malawi	2,564,338	.2	.01
Southern Africa, N.E.C.	1,169,279	.09	
Africa Total	1,198,950,456	100.00	3.53
Southern Africa Sub-region	540,936,094	45.1	1.59

Source: FT 455 US Exports, 1968 US Department of Commerce, Bureau of the Census.

*Here defined to include ten countries covered by the current National Security Study Memorandum; the three former High Commission Territories, South West Africa, the Republic of South Africa, Angola, Mozambique, Malawi, Rhodesia and Zambia.

US DIRECT INVESTMENT IN AFRICA
YEAR-END 1967
(in millions of dollars)

Countries	Mfctg.	Total	Share of Total US Direct Investment in Africa	Share of Total US Foreign Direct Investment
South Africa	303	667	29.3%	1.1%
Libya	N.A.	456	20.0%	0.8%
Liberia	N.A.	173	7.7%	0.3%
Total Africa	369	2,277	100.0%	3.8%

Source: Survey of Current Business, October 1968. Figures pertain to the book value of direct US investments only.

Annex 10

UNITED STATES MISSION TO THE
UNITED NATIONS

For release on delivery   Press Release No. 4233
Check text against
   delivery   August 2, 1963

Statement by Ambassador Adlai E. Stevenson,
United States Representative, in the Security
Council on the South African Question.

Mr. President

   All of us sitting here today know the melancholy
truth about the racial policies of the Government
of South Africa. Our task now is to consider what
further steps we can take to induce that government to remove the evil business of apartheid,
not only from our agenda, but from the continent
of Africa.
   The policy of apartheid denies the worth and
the dignity of the human person. And for this
very reason we must try to express our feelings,
we believe, with as much restraint as we can
muster. Self-righteousness is no substitute for
practical results.
   It is all too true that there is scarcely a
society of the world that is not touched by some
form of discrimination. Who among us can cast
the first stone or boast that we are free of any
semblance of discrimination, by color or religion or in some other form?
   I take the liberty of quoting to you a few
lines from a speech I made in Geneva a couple of
weeks ago. I said that:

      "In my country too many of our Negro citi-
      zens still do not enjoy their full civil
      rights - because ancient attitudes stubbornly

resist change in spite of the vigorous official policy of the government. But such
indignities are an anachronism that no progressive society can tolerate, and the last
vestiges must be abolished with all possible
speed. Actually in the past few years we have
made more progress in achieving full equality
of rights and opportunities for all of our
citizens than during any comparable period
since Abraham Lincoln's Proclamation of
Emancipation" - 100 years ago - "freed our
Republic and our national conscience from a
heavy burden.

"The very struggles which now call world-
wide attention to our shame are themselves
signs of a progress that will be increasingly
visible in the months ahead. The sound and
fury about racial equality that fill our
press and air waves are the sounds of the
great thaw; the log jam of the past is
breaking up."

I wanted to repeat what I said in Geneva to
leave no doubt that the United States position
is not one of self-righteousness, self-satis-
faction.

The question before us, however, is how and
when the log jam of racial discrimination will
be loosened and brought into the mainstream of
the United Nations Charter. If we all suffer
from the disease of discrimination in various
forms, at least most of us recognize the disease
for what it is - a disfiguring blight.

The whole point is that in many countries
governmental policies are dedicated to rooting
out this dread syndrome of prejudice and discrimination, while in South Africa we see the
anachronistic spectacle of the Government of a
great people which persists in seeing the
disease as the remedy, prescribing for the malady
of racism the bitter toxic of apartheid.

Mr. President, just as my country is determined to wipe out discrimination in our society
it will support efforts to bring about a change
in South Africa. It is in the United States' interest to do this; it is in the interest of
South Africa; it is in the interest of a world

which has suffered enough from bigotry, and prejudice and hatred.

The past two decades have seen an explosion of nationhood unequalled in history. Certainly the pace of decolonization in Africa has been nothing less than phenomenal, and it offers a record of progress far beyond what the most optimistic among us could have expected in 1945. The new states of Africa are gaining strength, resolutely fighting to build prosperous, dynamic societies and to do this in cooperation with other African states.

But as this meeting of the Security Council so graphically emphasizes, the full potential of this new era cannot be realized because of South Africa's self-chosen isolation. Worse yet, progress in Africa is over shadowed by the racial bitterness and resentment caused by the policies of the South African Government. And it is the duty of this Council to do what it can to insure that this situation does not deteriorate further, and that the injustice of apartheid comes to an end - not in bloodshed and bondage but in peace and freedom.

What we see and hear, however, offers us at present little hope. Indeed, the situation is worse than it was three years ago when this Council first met on the question of apartheid. Speakers before me have reviewed the record of previous discussions of apartheid by this Council and of the General Assembly. As they have pointed out, we have called repeatedly upon the Government of South Africa to consider world opinion, to cooperate with the United Nations, and to set in motion some meaningful steps toward ending discrimination, and policies and practices that would offend the whole world wherever they were pursued.

Outside of this organization, many members - not the least of which is my own government - have attempted repeatedly to persuade the South African Government to begin moving along the lines of these resolutions.

I myself, Mr. President, have had something emphatic to say on this score on two occasions in the Republic of South Africa; things that had grieved me to have to say after enjoying so much courtesy and hospitality from the friendly and the gracious people of that lovely land.

But it is only stating a fact of life to say that the visible result of all of these discussions and resolutions here in the United Nations and all diplomatic activity so far is zero.

It is only stating the obvious to say that up until this time our efforts have yielded no tangible results.

It is only calling things by their right name to say that we are confronted for the moment with a deadlock between the overwhelming majority of mankind and the Republic of South Africa.

There has been no forward motion; indeed, there has been retrogression – calculated retrogression.

Need I read the bill of particulars?

For the past fifteen years the Government of South Africa has built a barrier between the races – piling new restrictions upon old restrictions.

All South African must carry indentification cards, indicating racial ancestry.

Segregation in religion, education, and public accommodation is total.

Freedom of employment is limited; wage rates for the same work and the same responsibility are different according to the color of your skin.

Freedom of movement is inhibited.

Strikes by Africans in South Africa are illegal.

Africans in South Africa are prohibited from residing, from doing business or acquiring real property in most cities, and in large areas of the countryside.

Voters are registered on separate rolls according to race; and since 1958 non-European voters have had no representation whatever – even by Europeans – in the legislature.

This is not the whole story. But the point is that these and other measures of discrimination – aimed at the total separation of races into privileged and unprivileged segments of society – do not represent inherited social defects for which remedies are being sought but injustices deliberately and systematically imposed in the recent past.

Mr. President, we are all agreed and we have

176

proclaimed again and again in this body and in the General Assembly, and in many other forums of the United Nations, certain basic views about the issue before us. However, we must restate them again and again so that we can sum up where we stand and deliberate with clarity and candor on how to move forward.

First, we have affirmed and reaffirmed that apartheid is abhorrent. Our belief in the self-evident truths about human equality is enshrined in the Charter. Apartheid and racism – despite all of the tortured rationalizations we have heard from the apologists – are incompatible with the moral, the social and the constitutional foundations of our societies.

A second basic principle on which we are agreed is that all members of the organization have pledged themselves to take action, in co-operation with the organization, to promote observance of human rights without distinction as to race.

Thirdly, we continue to believe that this matter is of proper and legitimate concern to the United Nations. We have often stated in the General Assembly our belief that the Assembly can properly consider questions of racial discrimination and other violations of human rights where they are a Member's official policy and are inconsistent with the obligations of that member under Articles 55 and 56 of the Charter to promote observance of human rights without distinction as to race. Moreover, the apartheid policy of South Africa has clearly led to a situation the continuance of which is likely to endanger international peace and security.

We also believe that all members, in the words of the resolution passed almost unanimously by the Sixteenth General Assembly should take such separate and collective action to bring about an abandonment of apartheid as is open to them in conformity with the Charter. The United States supported that resolution and has complied with it.

I should like to take this occasion to bring up to date the record of the measures the United States has taken to carry out this purpose.

First, we have continued and, indeed, have accelerated our official representations to the Government of South Africa on all aspects of apartheid in that country. We have done this through public words and private diplomacy, expressing our earnest hope that the South African Government would take steps to reconsider and to revise its racial policies and to extend the full range of civic rights and opportunities to non-whites in the life of their country. And we have observed to the South African Government that in the absence of an indication of change, the United States would not cooperate in matters which would lend support to South Africa's present racial policies.

We have utilized our diplomatic and consular establishments in South Africa to demonstrate by words and by deeds our official disapproval of apartheid.

And as the United States Representatives informed the Special Political Committee of the General Assembly on October 19, 1962, the United States has adopted and is enforcing the policy of forbidding the sale to the South African Government of arms and military equipment, whether from government or commercial sources, which could be used by that government to enforce apartheid either in South Africa or in the administration of Southwest Africa. We have carefully screened both government and commercial shipments of military equipment to make sure that this policy is rigorously enforced.

But I am now authorized to inform the Security Council of still another important step which my government is prepared to take.

We expect to bring to an end the sale of all military equipment to the Government of South Africa by the end of this calendar year in order further to contribute to a peaceful solution and to avoid any steps which might at this point directly contribute to international friction in the area. There are existing contracts which provide for limited quantities of strategic equipment for defense against external threats, such as air-to-air missiles and torpedoes for submarines. We must honor these contracts.

The Council should be aware that in announcing

178

this policy, the United States as a nation with many responsibilities in many parts of the world, naturally reserves the right in the future to interpret this policy in the light of requirements for assuring the maintenance of international peace and security. If the interests of the world community require the provision of equipment for use in the common defense effort, we would naturally feel able to do so without violating the spirit and the intent of this resolve.

Now, Mr. President, we are taking this further step to indicate the deep concern which the Government of the United States feels at the failure of the Republic of South Africa to abandon its policy of apartheid.

In pursuing this policy, the Republic of South Africa, as we have so often said, is failing to discharge its obligations under Articles 55 and 56 of the Charter whereby members pledge themselves to take joint and separate action in cooperation with the organization for the achievement of, among other things, universal respect for the observance of human rights and fundamental freedoms for all without distinction as to race, sex, language or religion.

Stopping the sale of arms to South Africa emphasizes our hope that the Republic of South Africa will now reassess its attitude towards apartheid in the light of the constantly growing international concern at its failure to heed the numerous appeals made to it by various organs of the United Nations, as well as appeals of member states, such as my government.

As to the action of this Council in this proceeding, we are prepared to consult with other members and with the African Foreign Ministers present at the table and we will have some suggestions to make. It is clear to my delegation that the application of sanctions under Chapter VII in the situation now before us would be both bad law and bad policy.

It would be bad law because the extreme measures provided in Chapter VII were never intended and cannot reasonably be interpreted to apply to situations of this kind. The founders of the United Nations were very careful to reserve the right of the organization to employ mandatory coercive measures to situations where there was an actuality of international violence – or such a clear and present threat to the peace as to leave no reasonable alternative but resort to coercion. We do not have that kind of a situation here. Fortunately for all of us, there is still time to work out a solution through measures of pacific settlement, and any solution adopted by this Council must be reasonably calculated to promote such settlement.

It is bad policy because the application of sanctions in this situation is not likely to bring about the practical results that we seek, that is, the abandonment of apartheid. Far from encouraging the beginning of a dialogue between the Government of South Africa and its African population, punitive measures would only provoke intransigence and harden the existing situation.

Furthermore, the result of the adoption of such measures, particularly if compliance is not widespread and sincere, would create doubts about the validity of and diminish respect for the authority of the United Nations and the efficacy of the sanction process envisioned in the Charter. Also on this matter, views differ so widely that we cannot hope to agree on the necessary consensus to make such action effective even if it were legitimate and appropriate.

And as for suggestions of diplomatic isolation, persuasion cannot be exercised in a vacuum: conflicting views cannot be reconciled in absentia.

Instead we believe still further attempts should be made to build a bridge of communication, discussion and persuasion. If the human race is going to survive on this earth, wisdom, reason and right must prevails. And let us not forget that there are many wise and influential people in that great country who share our views.

It is regrettable accomplishments in so many fields of human endeavor in South Africa are being obscured by a racial policy repugnant to Africa and to the world. Certainly one ultimate goal for all of us is to assist South Africa to rejoin the African continent and to assist in the development of all the peoples of Africa.

And this, Mr. President, is why my government has looked with such favor on the idea of appointing special representatives of the Security Council who can work energetically and persistently and be free to exercise their own ingenuity and to pursue every prospect and every hint of a useful opening.

We cannot accept the proposition that the only alternative to apartheid is bloodshed.

We cannot accept the conclusion that there is no way out - no direction to go except the present collision course toward ultimate disaster in South Africa.

Certainly there are alternatives: and they must be identified and they must be explored before it is to late.

It is a matter of considerable regret to my delegation that the Government of South Africa has chosen to absent inself from these proceedings. But regrets to the side, Mr. President, it is exceedingly difficult in this shrunken and interdependent world to live in self-ostracism from international society: in this world of instant communication, it is progressively more hazardous to fly in the face of world opinion. And certainly the obligation to talk about dangerous disputes is too solemn to be ignored by even the most stubborn of leaders today.

Mr. President, there is nothing inherently immutable in any impasse in human affairs. Many a seemingly hopeless cause has prevailed in the course of history. I had occasion just last week to recall here that negotiations over the testing of nuclear weapons looked hopeless for five long, dreary and frustrating years - until the impasse was broken suddenly to the vast relief of an anxious world. And as I said, the stalemate was broken because men refused to give up hope, because men declined to give in to despair, because men worked consistently and doggedly to break the deadlock. Manifestly this treaty does not solve all of the problems in connection with nuclear armaments; but every long journey begins with a single step, and this is a beginning.

So I should like to suggest very emphatically that we approach the problem of apartheid in South Africa as a similar challenge to ingenuity, to the instinct for survival of humankind. As President Kennedy said with reference to the atomic treaty, we must not be afraid to test our hopes.

It is in the spirit of testing our hopes that this sad episode will end in reason and not in flame that I on behalf of my government solemnly, earnestly appeal to the Government of South Africa to change course and embark on a policy of national reconciliation and emancipation.

Appendix A

EXTRACTS FROM
THE PRESIDENTIALLY-CENSORED
HOUSE REPORT ON THE CIA,
JANUARY 19, 1976*

Angola

For reasons not altogether clear, and despite the opposition of senior government officials, the US has been heavily involved in the current civil war in Angola.

The CIA has informed the Committee that since January 1975, it had expended over $31 million in military hardware, transportation costs, and cash payments by the end of 1975. The Committee has reason to believe that the actual US investment is much higher. Information supplied to the Committee also suggests that the military intervention of the Soviet Union and Cuba is in large part a reaction to US efforts to break a political stalemate, in favor of its clients.

The beneficiaries of US aid are two of the three contesting factions: the National Front for the Independence of Angola (FNLA) and the National Union for the Total Independence of Angola (UNITA). The third faction contesting for control of the government, following independence on November 11, 1975, is the Soviet-backed Popular Movement for the Liberation of Angola (MPLA). CIA estimates that the fighting had claimed several thousand casualties by the end of 1975.

The main US client is the National Front, headed by Holden Roberto, a longtime associate and relative of President Mobutu Sese Seko

---

* "The CIA Report the President Doesn't Want You to Read," *The Village Voice*, February 16, 1976, p. 85.

of neighboring Zaire. Subsequent to President Mobutu's request last winter to Dr. Kissinger, as independence for Angola became a certainty and liberation groups began to jockey for position, the Forty Committee approved furnishing Roberto $300,000 for various political action activities,[474] restricted to non-military objectives.

Later events have suggested that this infusion of US aid, unprecedented[475] and massive in the underdeveloped colony, may have panicked the Soviets into arming their MPLA clients, whom they had backed for over a decade and who were now in danger of being eclipsed by the National Front. Events in Angola took a bellicose turn as the US was requested by President Mobutu to make a serious military investment.

In early June, 1975, CIA prepared a proposal paper for military aid to pro-US elements in Angola, the cost of which was set at $6 million. A revised program, costing $14 million, was approved by the Forty Committee and by President Ford in July. This was increased to $25 million in August, and to about $32 million in November. By mid-summer, it was decided that US aid should not be given solely to Roberto, but instead, divided between him and UNITA's Jonas Savimbi.

The Committee has learned that a task force composed of high US experts on Africa[477] strongly opposed military intervention; instead, last April they called for diplomatic efforts to encourage a political settlement among the three factions to avert bloodshed. Apparently at the direction of National Security Council aides, the task force recommendation was removed from the report and presented to NSC members as merely one policy option. The other two alternatives were a hands-off policy or substantial military intervention.

Of CIA's $31 million figure, said to represent expenditures to the end of 1975, about half is attributed to supply of light arms, mortars, ammunition, vehicles, boats, and communication equipment. The balance includes shipping expenses and cash payments. The Committee has reason to question the accuracy of CIA's valuation of military equipment sent to Angola.

A staff accountant on loan from the General Accounting Office has determined that CIA "costing" procedures and the use of surplus equipment have resulted in a substantial understatement of the value of US aid. Examples include .45 caliber automatic weapons "valued" by CIA at $5.00 each and .30 caliber semi-automatic carbines at $7.55. Based on a sampling of ordnance cost figures and a comparison with Department of Defense procedures, staff advises that the CIA's ordnance figure should at least be doubled.

Dr. Kissinger has indicated that US military intervention in Angola is based on three factors: Soviet support of the MPLA and the USSR's increased presence in Africa, US policy to encourage moderate independence groups in southern Africa, and the US interest in promoting the stability of Mobutu and other leadership figures in the area. Past support to Mobutu, along with his responsiveness to some of the United States recent diplomatic needs for Third World support, make it equally likely that the paramount factor in the US involvement is Dr. Kissinger's desire to reward and protect African leaders in the area. The US's expressed opposition to the MPLA is puzzling in view of Director Colby's statement to the Committee that there are scant ideological differences among the three factions, all of whom are nationalists above all else.[481]

Control of resources may be a factor. Angola has significant oil deposits and two American multinationals, Gulf and Texaco, operate in the off-shore area. Gulf had deposited some $100 million in concession fees in a national bank now under MPLA control. At the suggestion of the US government, the company suspended further payments.

Until recently, the US-backed National Front was supported by the People's Republic of China, which had provided about 100 military advisors. Mobutu has provided a staging area for US arms shipments and has periodically sent Zairois troops, trained by the Republic of North Korea, into Angola to support Roberto's operations. Small numbers of South African forces have been in the country and are known to have been in contact with Savimbi's UNITA troops.

Pursuant to Section 662 of the Foreign Assistance Act of 1974, the President has found that the Angola action program is "important to the national security." As directed by the Act, CIA has briefed the Congressional oversight committees as to the Forty Committee approvals of increased amounts of military aid.

CIA officials have testified to the Committee that there appears to be little hope of an outright MPLA military defeat. Instead, US efforts are now aimed at promoting a stalemate, and in turn, the cease-fire and the coalition government urged by the long-forgotten NSC task force.

---

474.   The political action program included the distribution of 50,000 campaign-type buttons identifying the wearer as a supporter of Roberto's FNLA.

475.   The United States has found itself in similar situations on other occasions. Having supported colonial power policies in previous years, they are constrained from developing a rapport with indigenous independence movements. The Soviets, however, are not similarly inhibited. Once the colonial power relinquishes control, the well-organized, well-financed, Soviet backed group is ready to step into the breach. The United States is forced at that point to scurry around looking for a rival faction or leader to support. The US has often chosen leaders who had a prior relationship with the colonial power and whose nationalist credentials are thus somewhat suspect, or leaders who have spent most of their time outside the country waiting for

the colonial power to depart. The point is that many of the US-backed groups begin with a variety of factors working to their disadvantage.

477.   The task force was composed of African experts within the Department of State, DoD officials, CIA officials, and others. Officials from the Department of State have told this Committee that the majority of that task force recommended diplomatic efforts to encourage a political settlement rather than intervention. After they had prepared their report for the Secretary of State containing this recommendation, they were informed by National Security Council aides that it was improper for them to make a recommendation on policy. Instead, they were instructed to simply list diplomatic efforts as one option among many in their final report. Thus, the African experts who made up the task force were not allowed to place their recommendations on paper to be reviewed by the Forty Committee.

481.   The Committee attempted to determine the difference between the three contesting factions in Angola. Mr. Colby responded to questions of that nature: "They are all independents. They are all for black Africa. They are all for some fuzzy kind of social system, you know, without really much articulation, but some sort of let's not be exploited by the capitalist nations." The Committee also attempted to discern why certain nations were supporting different groups if they were all similar in outlook:

"MR. ASPIN. And why are the Chinese backing the moderate group?

"MR. COLBY. Because the Soviets are backing the MPLA is the simplest answer.

"MR. ASPIN. It sounds like that is why we are doing it.

"MR. COLBY. It is."

Appendix B

EXCERPTS FROM
THE SPEECH DELIVERED BY
SECRETARY HENRY A. KISSINGER
IN LUSAKA, ZAMBIA,
APRIL 27, 1976*

Rhodesia

The United States is totally dedicated to seeing to it that the majority becomes the ruling power in Rhodesia . . . .United States policy for a just and durable Rhodesian solution will therefore rest on 10 elements:

First, the United States declares its support in the strongest terms for the proposal made by British Prime Minister Callaghan on March 22 of this year; that independence must be preceded by majority rule which, in turn, must be achieved no later than two years following the expeditious conclusion of negotiations.

Second, the Salisbury regime must understand that it cannot expect United States support either in diplomacy or in material help at any stage in its conflict with African states or African liberation movements.

Third, the United States will take steps to fulfill completely its obligation under international law to mandatory economic sanctions against Rhodesia. We will urge the Congress this year to repeal the Byrd Amendment.

---

* "Southern Africa and the United States: An Agenda for Cooperation." A Speech by Secretary Henry A. Kissinger delivered at a luncheon in his honor hosted by President Kenneth Kaunda in Lusaka, Zambia, April 27, 1976. Washington, DC: US Department of State, Bureau of Public Affairs, April 27, 1976 (PR 205).

Fourth . . . the United States, on the conclusion of my consultations in black Africa, will communicate clearly and directly to the Salisbury regime our view of the urgency of a rapid negotiated settlement leading to majority rule.

Fifth, the United States will . . . inform American citizens that we have no official representation in Rhodesia nor any means of providing them with assistance or protection. American travelers will be advised against entering Rhodesia; American residents there will be urged to leave.

Sixth . . . steps should be taken — in accordance with the recent UN Security Council resolution — to assist Mozambique, whose closing of its borders with Rhodesia to enforce sanctions has imposed upon it a great additional economic hardship . . . . The United States is willing to provide $12.5 million of assistance.

Seventh, the United States — together with other members of the United Nations — is ready to help alleviate economic hardship for any countries neighboring Rhodesia which decide to enforce sanctions by closing their frontiers.

Eighth . . . the United States will consider sympathetically requests for assistance for these refugees by the UN High Commissioner for Refugees or other appropriate international organizations.

Ninth . . . we are ready to join with other interested nations in a program of economic, technical and educational assistance, to enable an independent Zimbabwe to achieve the progress and the place in the community of nations.

Finally, we state our conviction that whites as well as blacks should have a secure future and civil rights in Zimbabwe that has achieved racial justice. A constitutional structure should protect minority rights together with establishing majority rule. We are prepared to devote some of our assistance programs to this objective.

Namibia

We reiterate our call upon the South African Government to permit all the people and groups of Namibia to express their views freely, under UN supervision, on the political future and constitutional structure of their country.

We urge the South African Government to announce a definite timetable acceptable to the world community for the achievement of self-determination.

The United States is prepared to work with the international community, and especially with African leaders, to determine what further steps would improve prospects for a rapid and acceptable transition to Namibian independence.

Once concrete movement toward self-determination is underway, the United States will ease its restrictions on trade and investment in Namibia. We stand ready to provide economic and technical assistance to help Namibia take its rightful place among the independent nations of the world.

South Africa

A peaceful end to institutionalized inequality is in the interest of all South Africans. The United States will continue to encourage and work for peaceful change. Our policy toward South Africa is based upon the premise that within a reasonable time we shall see a clear evolution toward equality of opportunity and basic human rights for all South Africans. The United States will exercise all its efforts in that direction.